CW01429224

How to Avoid Landlord Taxes

Tax busting tips to help boost your property profits!

By

Arthur Weller & Amer Siddiq

Publisher Details
This guide is published by Tax Portal Ltd. 3 Sanderson Close, Great Sankey, Warrington, Cheshire, WA5 3LN.

'How to Avoid Landlord Taxes' – First published in May 2009. Second Edition April 2010. Third Edition July 2010. Fourth Edition April 2011. Fifth Edition April 2012. Sixth Edition April 2013. Seventh edition May 2014. Eighth edition April 2015. Ninth Edition April 2016

Copyright
The right of Arthur Weller and Tax Portal Ltd to be identified as the authors of this guide has been asserted in accordance with the Copyright, Designs and Patents Act 1988, England.

© 2009-2016 Arthur Weller and Tax Portal Ltd

A CIP Copy of this book is available from the British Library.

978-0-9932513-2-0

All rights reserved
All rights reserved. No part of this guide may be reproduced or transmitted in any form or by any means, electronically or mechanically, including photocopying, recording or any information storage or retrieval system, without prior permission in writing from the publisher.

Permission is granted to print a single hardcopy version of this guide for your personal use only.

Trademarks
Property Tax Portal, Tax Portal Ltd and other Tax Portal Ltd services/ products referenced in this guide are registered trademarks or trademarks of Tax Portal Ltd in the UK and/or other countries.

Disclaimer

1. This guide is produced for General guidance only, and professional advice should be sought before any decision is made. Individual circumstances can vary and therefore no responsibility can be accepted by the author, Arthur Weller, or the publisher Tax Portal Ltd, for any action taken, or any decision made to refrain from action, by any readers of this guide.

2. Tax rules and legislation are constantly changing and therefore the information printed in this guide is correct at the time of printing – April 2016.

3. Neither the author nor Tax Portal Ltd offer financial, legal or investment advice. If you require such advice then, we urge you to seek the opinion of an appropriate professional in the relevant field. We care about your success and therefore encourage you to take appropriate advice before you put any of your financial or other resources at risk. Don't forget, investment values can decrease as well as increase.

4. To the fullest extent permitted by law, Arthur Weller and Tax Portal Ltd do not accept liability for any direct, indirect, special, consequential or other losses or damages of whatsoever kind arising from using this guide.

   The guide itself is provided 'as is' without express or implied warranty.

5. Arthur Weller and Tax Portal Ltd reserve the right to alter any part of this guide at any time without notice

Contents

About the Authors

Some words about the authors of this unique guide, bringing together a property tax specialist and a property investor!

Arthur Weller - The Property Tax Specialist

Arthur Weller is a tax specialist who advises other accountants. He is one of the most knowledgeable and respected tax specialists in the country.

He is also the lead technical tax specialist and design consultant for www.property-tax-portal.co.uk.

Arthur is based in the northwest and qualified in 1997 as a certified accountant in a small firm of accountants. They specialised to a degree in property, and he worked for some years in their tax department.

He then moved on to a medium-sized firm, where he was the technical manager in the tax department.

In 1998 he passed the exams of the Institute of Taxation, and in June 2000 he left to set up his own tax consultancy.

Arthur works mainly in an advisory capacity for accountants in all areas of taxation. He also runs a telephone help line, giving phone advice on all areas of taxation to accountants around the country.

Much of his work has been focused in the following areas:

- property taxation (Arthur is regarded as a property tax specialist);
- capital gains tax;
- stamp duty;
- income tax;
- company tax;

Amer Siddiq - The Landlord

First and foremost Amer Siddiq is a UK landlord/property investor. He is passionate about all aspects of property investment and over the last nine years has grown a portfolio in the northwest of England

As well as growing a portfolio and speaking in public at various property investment events, Amer has also brought to market a number of websites to help landlords to better manage and grow their portfolios whilst reducing their taxes.

These include:

Property Portfolio SOFTWARE	**Property Portfolio Software** UK's leading and triple award winning PC based property management software. Helps landlords to get better organised in every aspect of their property business. Visit: www.propertyportfoliosoftware.co.uk
landlord vision	**Landlord Vision** Our next generation landlord software solution that runs in the cloud. **Take your 30 day FREE Trial today.** Visit: www.landlordvision.co.uk
TAXINSIDER	**Tax Insider** A website providing monthly tax newsletters to help UK tax payers minimise their taxes. Visit: www.taxinsider.co.uk

Acknowledgements

Lee Sharpe, Chartered Tax Advisor and author of:

- Tax DOs and DON'Ts for Property Companies,
- Tax Secrets for Property Developers and Renovators

Both books can be purchased through www.property-tax-portal.co.uk website.

Lee is also a public speaker and provides valuable tax expertise to the www.property-tax-portal.co.uk and www.taxinsider.co.uk websites.

Daniel Feingold, International Law and Tax Specialist. Daniel is a rarity amongst tax specialists as not only is he a much sought after international tax specialist but he is also a barrister. He is also the international tax editor for www.property-tax-portal.co.uk.

Jennifer Adams, property tax specialist with a flair for helping clients to structure their affairs in a tax efficient manner. Jennifer has contributed the major section on Trusts and various other smaller sections throughout. Jennifer is also a senior tax writer for the tax magazines available at www.taxinsider.co.uk.

1. The Importance of Tax Planning

We all instinctively do some tax planning in our daily lives, even if it is simply remembering to buy our "duty frees" when we return from our holiday abroad.

If you are going to make the best of your property business, then you need to be alert to the tax implications of your business plans, and to any opportunities to reduce the likely tax bill. Your instinct may be enough for your duty free goodies, but for tax on your business, you need a more structured approach!

"Tax planning" means arranging your business affairs so that you pay the minimum amount of tax that the law requires. It does not mean trying to conceal things from the Taxman, and it does not mean indulging in highly complex (and expensive!) artificial "tax avoidance" schemes.

"Every man is entitled if he can to order his affairs so that the tax attaching under the appropriate Acts is less than it would otherwise be." That is what the House of Lords said in 1935, when they found for the Duke of Westminster and against the Inland Revenue. This still holds true today, though there is now a mass of "anti-avoidance" legislation to consider when thinking about tax planning – and before you ask, the Duke's tax planning idea was stopped by anti-avoidance legislation!

1.1. Knowing When to Consider Planning

A question you will most certainly ask yourself is 'when should I consider tax planning for my property business?'

The short answer is "all the time", but to be realistic, no-one is likely to do this. The trick is to develop by experience, a sense of when a tax planning opportunity (or a potentially expensive tax pitfall) is likely to present itself.

You should consider tax planning in all of the following situations, for example:

1.1.1. Buying

If you are buying a property, you need to consider:

- Buying the property – It could be you as an individual, you and your spouse, you and a business partner, a Limited Company owned by you, or perhaps a Trust you have set up. Your decision will depend on your future business strategy

- Financing the property – You will need to consider whether you are taking out a mortgage, and if so how will it be secured. It may not always make sense to secure the loan on the property you are buying if you have other assets on which you can secure the loan.

- Plans for the property – It could be that you are you buying the property to sell it again in the short term, or to hold it long term and benefit from the rental income. The tax treatment will be different according to which is the case, and different planning should be done before the property is bought.

1.1.2. Repairs and refurbishment

If you spend money on a property, you need to consider:

- Whether you doing it in order to sell it again in the short term, or whether you will continue letting it.

- If the work being done is classed as a **repair** to the property, or an **improvement.** See icon below for the difference between the two.

  The distinction between a repair and an improvement to a property is very important, because although the cost of repairs can be deducted from your rental income for tax purposes, an improvement can only be claimed as a deduction against CGT when you sell the property.

  Essentially, a repair is when you replace like with like, whereas an improvement involves adding to the property (say, a conservatory or a loft conversion), or replacing something with something significantly better (say, removing the old storage heaters and installing oil-fired central heating).

  HMRC do not always behave logically when it comes to repairs versus improvements.

  James Bailey shares the following experience with us:

  "A client of mine sold a seaside property, in circumstances where he would have to pay CGT on the sale profit. He had spent a lot of money on this property, which when he bought it had not been touched since the early 1950s.

  He had ripped out the old "utility" kitchen, for example, and replaced it with a state-of –the –art designer affair in gleaming slate, chrome, and steel. The old 1950s cooker had had some bakelite knobs to turn the gas on and off – the new kitchen range had the computer power of the average 1970s space capsule.

  Clearly an improvement, and so deductible from his capital gain, but HMRC tried to argue that one kitchen is much like another and he was just replacing like with like – so they said it was a repair, which was no good to him in his case as there was no rental income from which he could deduct the cost of repairs."

1.1.3. Selling

When you decide to dispose of a property, there are other tax issues to consider:

- Who is the property going to? – If it is to someone "connected" with you, such as a close relative or a business partner, and if you do not charge them the full market value, HMRC can step in and tax you as if you had sold it for full value.

- Will you be paying CGT or income tax on the profit you make? – The planning opportunities are very different, depending on which tax is involved.

- What are the terms of the sale? Is it just a cash sale, or is the buyer a developer who is offering you a "slice of the action" in the form of a share of the profits from the development? There is important anti-avoidance legislation to consider if this is the case.

1.1.4. Life changes

Whenever your life undergoes some significant changes, you should consider tax planning.

Here are some examples when tax planning should be considered:

- Getting married – a married couple (and a civil partnership) have a number of tax planning opportunities denied to single people, but there are also one or two pitfalls to watch out for.

- Moving house – it is usually not a good idea to sell the old house immediately, as there are often tax advantages to keeping it and letting it out.

- Changing your job. You may become a higher or lower rate tax payer and this may mean you should change your tax strategy.

  If you are moving house, and you sell the old residence, you will have the cash left after you have paid off the mortgage and the various removal costs to spend on your new home. If you need a mortgage to buy the new home, the interest on that mortgage is not allowed as a deduction for tax purposes.

  If, instead, you remortgage the old house and let it out, ALL the mortgage interest you pay can be deducted against the rent you receive whatever you do with the cash you have released – and you may well be able to sell the house after three years of letting (or sometimes a longer period), and pay no CGT on the increased value since you stopped living there.

- Death – IHT is charged at 40% on the value of your estate when you die, to the extent that the value is greater than (for 2014/15) £325,000. By planning early enough it is possible to reduce the IHT burden considerably.

1.1.5. Politics

There are two occasions each year when you need to be particularly alert – the Pre Budget Report in November or December, and The Budget in March.

On both these occasions the Chancellor of the Exchequer announces tax rates, and new tax legislation, which might well affect you and your property business. In some cases, however, new tax legislation is announced at other times – it pays to keep a weather eye on the financial pages of the newspaper, or to subscribe to a magazine or journal that will alert you to important tax changes that may affect your business.

1.1.6. End and start of the tax year

The tax year ends on the 5th April each year and it is a good idea to review your tax situation before this date to make sure you are not missing any planning opportunities.

1.2. The Real Benefits of Tax Planning

Robert Kiyosaki, author of the number one bestselling book 'Rich Dad Poor Dad', says *'Every time people try to punish the rich, the rich don't simply comply, they react. They have the money, power and intent to change things. They do not sit there and voluntarily pay more taxes. They search for ways to minimize their tax burden'*

The whole purpose of tax planning is to save you tax and to put more profits in your pocket. That is why the rich are always looking at ways of beating the taxman, because they benefit from tax planning.

1.2.1. Paying less tax

When I (co-author Amer) started investing in property the challenge to me was not to just grow a property portfolio but to grow it in the most tax efficient way possible.

It soon dawned on me that implementing just the simplest of tax saving strategies was going to help me to make considerably more profits.

Don't fall into the trap where you only think about tax when you are considering selling or even worse after you have sold the property.

By taking tax advice at the right times and on a regular basis you will legitimately avoid or reduce taxes both in the short and the long term.

This means that you will have greater profits to spend as you wish.

1.2.2. Clear 'entrance' and 'exit' strategies

When you sit down and analyse properties that you are considering for investment, you will no doubt look at how much rental income the property will generate and what you expect to achieve in capital appreciation.

Knowing the estimated tax liabilities right from the outset will save you from any nasty surprises in the future.

> Your personal circumstances can change at a whim. The last thing that you want to do is fall into a situation where you are forced to sell a property but are unable to pay the taxman because you never considered your tax situation.

1.2.3. Staying focused

When you are deciding on the property investment strategies that you are going to adopt it is a good idea to talk them through with a tax adviser.

If your investment strategy changes then it is likely to have an impact on your tax strategy so it should be reviewed with your tax adviser.

Your tax strategy will go hand in hand with your investment strategy and will help you to keep focused on your property investment and financial goals.

1.2.4. Improving cash flow

One of the challenges that you will face as a property investor is cash flow. In other words, you need to make sure that you have enough money coming in from your property business to pay for all property related bills, maintenance and repairs, and of course tax on the rental profits.

> Remember, timing of expenditures can be the difference between a 'high' and a 'nil' tax bill. Therefore, keeping in regular contact with your tax adviser, especially when coming towards the end of the tax year can have a significant impact on your property cash flow.

1.2.5. Avoiding common tax traps

There are many tax traps that you can fall into if you have not taken any tax advice at all, not to mention the numerous great tax planning opportunities you will m ss out on too. In is not uncommon to hear stories about investors who have made a £100,000 profit on a single property and then sold it without taking any tax advice whatsoever. If you fall into this situation then you could be hit with a hefty tax bill.

It will hurt you even more if after selling you realise that you could have easily turned the tax liability to zero had you taken some simple tax advice.

Good tax advisers will know of the most common traps that you are likely to fall into, so a few minutes spent wisely could save you thousands in taxes.

1.3. Asking HMRC for Tax Advice

This strategy has been written by James Bailey.

This article is being written by request – apparently from time to time people tell the Tax Insider office that all the effort that goes into offering them tax advice is a waste of time, and tax consultants are also unnecessary, because you can simply telephone HM Revenue & Customs (HMRC) and get free advice. However, free advice is not always the best advice.

1.3.1. Making use of HMRC services

I am a great believer in getting advice from HMRC in some circumstances – for example, they operate a number of "clearance" services whereby you can set out the details of a proposed transaction for them, and they will tell you the tax consequences they believe will flow from it.

Some of these clearances are enshrined in statute – there are some quite draconian examples of anti-avoidance legislation which can also catch quite innocent commercial transactions, and there is a statutory process for obtaining HMRC's agreement in advance that they will not wheel out their sledgehammers to crack your innocent commercial nut.

There are also other informal HMRC clearance procedures which can be useful when you are considering a transaction where the tax treatment may turn on a matter of opinion, and it is useful to know HMRC's opinion in advance.

It is also possible to agree valuations of assets for capital gains tax purposes where these are needed to complete a tax return – much better to have the discussion before you put the return in than to hope for the best and submit it, only to have the same discussion as part of an HMRC "Aspect Enquiry" where the possibility of penalties looms if they consider your valuation was a little sloppy!

I use all these services frequently on behalf of my clients, and they are a great help in providing a better service for them. I could carp on about the delays that are sometimes involved, and the way that in some cases HMRC will use any argument they can to avoid expressing an opinion, but on the whole the service works smoothly.

1.3.2. The drawback

I suspect, however, that the "help" the punters who contact Tax Insider are referring to is the "help" you can get by ringing HMRC up while filling in your tax return, or when confronted by a tax situation that you do not understand. In some cases, no harm will result, and you may even get the right answer, but on the whole I am very nervous about this "Do it yourself" approach to tax.

HMRC's own policy on giving advice is contained in their "Code of Practice 10", and the following sentence from that document illustrates a major gap in their service:

"However, we will not help with tax planning, or advise on transactions designed to avoid or reduce the tax charge which might otherwise be expected to arise".

Fair enough – but I and my fellow tax consultants certainly will give you that advice, and for surprisingly modest fees, considering the savings you may be able to make!

1.3.3. A practical tip

There is a serious point here – HMRC do their best to promote the view that there is a "correct" amount of tax that is due as a result of any particular transaction, whereas in all but the simplest of cases, there are grey areas and the way a transaction is structured can make a big difference to the resulting tax bill.

As Lord Tomlin said in the House of Lords during the case of The Duke of Westminster v The Commissioners of Inland Revenue in 1936 ***"Every man is entitled if he can to order his affairs so that the tax attaching under the appropriate Acts is less than it would otherwise be"***.

That remains good law and seems to me a sensible way to deal with the State's demands for ever higher taxes, but don't expect HMRC to help you!

2. HMRC Let Property Campaign

Lee Sharpe looks at some key concepts that may help landlords to mitigate penalties in the 'let property campaign'.

There are different penalty regimes depending on whether or not the taxpayer already files a tax return; also penalty legislation was substantially re-worked in Finance Act 2007, basically for 2008/09 and later tax returns. For simplicity, we shall use the current terms, but much holds good for the old rules.

2.1. The Penalty Scale

Briefly, the penalty regime follows in order of gravity:

* non-culpable: reasonable excuse/reasonable care taken;
* non-deliberate/careless;
* deliberate; and
* deliberate and concealed.

The penalty rate increases going down the scale; there can be reductions where the taxpayer approaches HMRC first, and for actively helping HMRC to resolve the issue.

2.2. Is There A Tax Liability?

If a taxpayer has no additional tax to pay by reason of the letting activity then normally there should also be no penalty to pay.

2.2.1. 'Reasonable excuse'

Where the taxpayer has not told HMRC that he needs to file a tax return, there can be a 'late notification penalty' calculated by reference to the amount of tax which remained unpaid by the normal payment deadline for that year – normally 31 January following the relevant tax year. However, where the taxpayer has a 'reasonable excuse' for not having notified HMRC that a tax return was due, then there will be no penalty.

2.2.2. What is a 'reasonable excuse'?

Unfortunately, there is no legal definition, leaving HMRC and the courts some latitude in interpretation. Perhaps unsurprisingly, HMRC's position is more demanding than the courts'. HMRC's Compliance Handbook manual (at CH71540) says that 'a reasonable excuse is normally an unexpected or unusual event that is either unforeseeable or beyond the person's control, and which prevents the person from complying with an obligation to notify when they would otherwise have done'.

The Tribunals, however, disagree; for example, in Mr TJ Fisher (T/a The Crispin) v HMRC [2011] UKFTT 235:

"...As a matter of law, that is wrong. If Parliament had intended to say that a person could only avoid a penalty by establishing that an exceptional event or exceptional circumstance had arisen, it would have said so. Parliament chose to use the phrase 'reasonable excuse' which is an ordinary expression in everyday usage which must be given its natural meaning."

Broadly, if an ordinary person would find the taxpayer's excuse reasonable, that may suffice. A similar case, Perrin v Revenue & Customs [2014] UKFTT 488 (TC), also confirms this.

The Compliance Handbook manual (at CH17540) later states:

"Each [reasonable excuse] depends upon the particular circumstances in which the failure occurred and the particular circumstances and abilities of the person who has failed."

Essentially, the Perrin case also agrees with this. But note that the reasonable excuse must last up until the taxpayer takes steps to remedy the situation: once you have realised that a return is due, you must act reasonably quickly to file the return.

2.2.3. 'Reasonable care'

Where a taxpayer already files a tax return but has failed to include any (or all) rental profits, then this will constitute an inaccuracy in his or her tax return.

However, where the taxpayer has taken 'reasonable care' in preparing his return then, again, no penalty should be charged. The concept of 'reasonable care' is very similar to that for having a 'reasonable excuse' above. HMRC states (at CH81120):

"For example, we do not expect the same level of knowledge or expertise from a self-employed un-represented individual as we do from a large multinational company."

Examples of reasonable care in a tax return:

- a reasonably held view of what deductions might be claimed which is later shown to be incorrect;
- a minor calculation error which was too small to be obvious; and
- relying on HMRC's advice that proves to be wrong, despite having provided all relevant details.

2.2.4. Onus of proof

HMRC states (at CH84540):

"The onus is on the person to satisfy us that they took reasonable care to avoid inaccuracy."

However, the truth is that, in a tribunal, it is down to HMRC to prove that a return or other submission contains a careless or deliberate inaccuracy (CH81180). HMRC's old Appeals Handbook manual (at AH1325) discusses the onus of proof and confirms specifically for penalty appeals:

"When HMRC makes a penalty determination it is asserting that an offence has been committed. The onus of proof and evidential burden rest firmly with the Crown" (See also King v Walden [2001] EWHC Ch 419). It also goes on to say, "The more serious the accusation the higher the standard of proof must be."

This suggests that, to prove that a taxpayer's behaviour was deliberate, especially with steps to conceal his actions, the standard of proof is higher than for mere carelessness.

2.2.5. Was it deliberate, or can the penalty be suspended?

According to HMRC (see CH402705), deliberate behaviour is when a person knows that he is required to notify HMRC about a relevant obligation, is able to do so, but does not. In the context of the 'let property campaign', in 'Your Guide to Making a Disclosure', HMRC says (at 3.9 Penalties): "HMRC may find it difficult to accept... that someone in business for many years, earning significant amounts without telling HMRC, has not done so deliberately".

The higher thresholds (i.e., deliberate action) are important, not just because the penalties are higher, but because a penalty may not be 'suspended' for a taxpayer's deliberate failure to take reasonable care.

Where there is an inaccuracy in a tax return, the penalty may be suspended subject to conditions, for a probationary period (of up to two years) after which time, provided the taxpayer suffers no further inaccuracy penalties, the penalty is cancelled. The rationale is that, rather than simply punishing the taxpayer, suspension encourages future compliance.

The problem is that HMRC is quite reticent about suspending penalties – I can find no mention of them in the let property campaign – yet at CH83110 HMRC says:

"Whenever we decide that a person is liable to a penalty for a careless inaccuracy we must consider whether we can suspend it".

HMRC also often says that the penalty can be suspended only if the same error could be repeated in future, whereas the courts have found that this is incorrect: the purpose of suspension is to help prevent any further careless inaccuracy (Testa v HMRC [2013] UKFTT 151).

2.2.6. Conclusion – and a helping hand from HMRC?

Advice from a suitably qualified professional adviser is strongly recommended. Clearly, it makes sense to approach HMRC unprompted in any event, to minimise any penalties that may be due. If there is an opportunity to claim that there was a reasonable excuse for not notifying HMRC of any rental income, or that reasonable care was taken when submitting a tax return, then that should be explored.

Likewise, any opportunity for suspending a penalty should be carefully considered – even if HMRC has not. But that may require care to indicate that conduct was not deliberate, while bearing in mind that it should be for HMRC to prove at tribunal.

Knowing Your Property Tax Strategy

3. Understanding your Tax Liabilities

Over the past few years property investment has become a very profitable way to make money.

Unfortunately there are very few people who consider the tax implications of their investment strategy before they decide to invest. Instead they take a view that they will address the tax issues when they decide to dispose of the property. This can be a very costly mistake as some simple planning can help to avoid large tax bills in the future.

The table below gives an indication of the tax that may be due if you follow any of the popular strategies outlined below.

Strategy	Description	Income Tax	Capital Gains Tax
Buy-to-let	Probably the most popular investment method and a strategy for long-term investment. Income tax will be due on the annual rental profits and CGT due when the property is disposed of.	Yes	Yes
Develop & Sell	This is typically classed as a short-term (i.e. 3-6 months) investment and only Income Tax is due if you are trading in properties in this way. All property development related expenditures can be offset against the final selling price.	Yes	No
Develop & Rent	Another typical long-term investment, where the property is developed and then rented out. All capital expenditure incurred developing the property can be offset when the property is disposed.	Yes	Yes

	However rental profit will be subject to annual income tax.		
Buy & Sell	If you are a master or want to become a master of buying undervalued property and then re-selling at a higher price then you will be classed as a property trader and will typically be subject to Income Tax only.	Yes	No
Buy-let-live	A good investment strategy to make use of some very significant tax breaks if you are sitting on large capital gains. This strategy only really applies to investors who intent to hold only a small number of properties during their life-time i.e. (3-6 properties). Again income tax will be due on rental profits and CGT when the property is disposed of.	Yes	Yes (but is dramati-cally reduced)
Buy-live-let	Probably the most tax efficient way to avoid capital gains tax for the small investor. This increasingly popular strategy involves letting your previous main residence when buying a new home or moving abroad. Again income tax will be due on rental profits and CGT when the property is disposed of.	Yes	Yes (but is dramati-cally reduced)
Rent-a-Room	If you decide to rent-a-room that is part of your main residence then you can receive an annual rental income, to the value of £7,500 and not have any income tax liability. Ay income above this amount will be subject to income tax. CGT is not due if you sell your main residence which has been	Yes (if claiming rent-a-room relief and income is greater than £7,500)	No (if tenants live with the family owning the property)

	classed as your only home during the whole period of ownership. Please Note: if the tenants renting do not live together with the family, then there can be CGT on that part of the house rented out. See section 21 for more details		
Furnished Holiday Lets	If you let a furnished property as a holiday let, then you will be subject to income tax on any rental profits. There are number of very generous tax breaks available for those investing in Furnished Holiday Lets. See section 22 for more details	Yes	Yes

How to Slash your Property Income Tax

Before we look at the different income tax saving strategies, it is important to understand what is meant by the term **income tax** and when property investors and landlords are liable to pay it.

4.   Income Tax Liabilities for Investors/Traders

Anybody investing in property is liable to pay income tax on any profitable income that is generated from their properties.

There are two main categories of people who invest in property, and both are liable to pay income tax. The characteristics of each are detailed in the following sections.

4.1.   Property Investor

If you invest in property for the long term, i.e., you have buy-to-let properties, then you will be referred to as a **property investor** (more commonly known as a landlord). This is because you are holding on to a property for the long term.

If you are letting your investment properties, then you will be liable to pay income tax annually on the rental profits.

It is also likely that you will have another source of income, unless you have a large portfolio of properties where the rental income funds your lifestyle.

4.2.   Property Traders/Dealers

If you are investing in property for the short term, i.e., 6–12 months, and intend to sell with the aim of generating a dealing profit, then you will be referred to as **property dealer** or **property trader**.

Property dealers and traders are liable to pay income tax when they sell the property.

You will find that most full-time property developers or renovators are classed as property dealers/traders.

4.3.   Income Tax Rates

You can use the following link to view the income tax rates for previous years:

http://www.hmrc.gov.uk/rates/it.htm

The current rates of income tax for the 2016–2017 tax year are detailed in the table below:

INCOME TAX 2016–2017

Rate	Band	Description
Nil	£0 to £11,000	The first £11,000 of each individual's income is Tax Free.
20%	£11,001 to £43,000	The next £32,000 is taxed at 20%.
40%	£43,001 to £100,000	The next £57,000 is taxed at 40%.
60%	£100,001 to £122,000	The next £22,000 is taxed at 60%. This is because of the withdrawal of the Personal Allowance.
40%	£ 122,001 to 150,000	The next £28,000 is taxed at 40%.
45%	> £150,000	Anything above £150,000 is taxed at 45%

The above table assumes that the personal allowance is £11,000. It also disregards the 0% tax rate on savings income for the first £5,000.

4.4. Income Tax Calculation Case Studies

Here are some case studies to illustrate how the tax liability is calculated for property investors and property dealers/traders.

4.4.1. Income Tax Calculation for Property Investors

The case study below illustrates the income tax liability for a basic-rate taxpayer.

Income Tax Calculation for Property Investor (1)

John works as a local government officer and receives an annual salary of £20,000. He buys a property close to his local hospital for £95,000. He receives a monthly rental income of £600.

The property is let for the whole 2016–2017 tax year, which means that he has received an annual rental income of £7,200.

In the tax year he has also incurred property-related expenses of £2,000.

These expenditures are made up as follows:

Expense	Amount
Interest repaid on mortgage	£1,200
Plumbing (to fix water leak)	£150
Annual gas safety inspection	£100
Central heating maintenance contract	£300
Replacement door fitted	£250
Total Expenditure	£2,000

This means that John's taxable rental profit is £5,200 (i.e., £7,200 – £2,000).

On this amount he is liable to pay tax at 20%. This is because his £5,200 rental profit falls into the basic rate band.

Therefore his tax liability is **£1,040** on the £5,200 profit.

The following case study illustrates how the rental income from the property pushes John into the higher-rate tax band.

Income Tax Calculation for Property Investor (2)

This is the same scenario as in the previous case study. The only difference is that John has an annual salary of £42,500.

John's tax liability on the £5,200 profit is now calculated as follows.

The first £500 is taxed at the basic rate of 20%.

The remaining £4,700 is taxed at the higher rate of 40%. This is because the rental profit has taken his total income into the higher-rate tax band.

Therefore his tax liability is as follows:

$$(£500 \times 0.2) \quad + \quad (£4,700 \times 0.4)$$
$$£100 \quad + \quad £1,880$$

$$= \quad £1.980$$

John's tax liability is **£1,980** on the £5,200 profit.

4.4.2. Income Tax Calculation for Property Developers

It is important to remember that if you become a property dealer, then this is a new self-employed trade and you are liable for Class 4 National Insurance (NI) on the profits as well as for Class 2 NI. See HMRC leaflet SE1 Thinking of working for yourself:
www.gov.uk/government/uploads/system/uploads/attachment_data/file/366588/se1.pdf.

In order to make the case studies in this section easier to understand the NI contributions have not been calculated.

The following case study illustrates how the income tax liability is calculated for a part-time property dealer.

Income Tax Calculation for Property Dealer (1)

Bill works as a local government officer and earns a salary of £25,000. Bill wants to become a property developer, so he buys a run-down property for £50,000 in December 2015.

He spends £20,000 renovating and re-decorating the property before selling it six months later for £95,000.

This gives him a taxable profit of £25,000 (i.e. selling price – (purchase price + costs incurred on the property)).

Bill's tax liability on the £25,000 profit is made in the 2016–2017 tax year, so his tax liability is calculated as follows.

The first £18,000 is taxed at the basic rate of 20%.

The remaining £7,000 is taxed at the higher rate of 40%. This is because the property development profit has taken his total income into the higher-rate tax band.

Therefore his tax liability is as follows:

(£18,000 × 0.2)	+	(£7,000 × 0.4)
£3,600	+	£2,800
	=	£6,400

Bill's tax liability is **£6,400** on the £25,000 profit.

The following case study illustrates how the income tax liability is calculated for a full-time property dealer.

Income Tax Calculation for Property Dealer (2)

Robert, a colleague of Bill and John, resigns from his job in the local government and decides to become a full-time property dealer.

In his first year of dealing he buys two properties, renovates them, and sells them for a profit of £55,000 each. This means that he has a taxable income of £110,000. The profit is made in the 2016–2017 tax year, so his tax liability is calculated as follows.

- The first £11,000 is tax-free due to the personal allowance.
- The next £32,000 is taxed at the basic rate of 20%.
- The next £57,000 is taxed at the rate of 40%.
- The remaining £10,000 is taxed at the even higher rate of 60%.

Here is the tax calculation:

Tax Rate	Amount	Tax Liability
Nil	£11,000	£0
20%	£32,000	£6,400
40%	£57,000	£22,800
60%	£10,000	£6,000
Total Tax Liability		**£35,200**

Therefore Robert has a tax liability of **£35,200** on the £110,000 profit.

5. Owning Properties as a Sole Trader

Holding a property in a sole name can be tax beneficial under certain circumstances.

In this section we will get to grips with why people hold properties as a sole trader and will learn about some of the tax benefits and drawbacks of owning properties in this way.

5.1. Buying Properties as a Sole Trader

A **sole trader** is an individual who buys properties in his or her sole name.

Although it is still a very common way to purchase properties, it is not necessarily the most tax efficient.

In most cases, properties are usually purchased as a sole trader for non-tax-related reasons.

Here are the two most common non-tax-related reasons why you might decide to buy property as a sole trader.

a) You don't have a partner who you can invest with.

b) You don't want to invest with anybody else; that is, you can't trust anybody, or you want total control over your investment.

If you have invested for either of these reasons, then you can still make tax savings.

5.2. When is it Tax Efficient to Buy Property as a Sole Trader?

The ideal scenario for buying a property as a sole trader is if you have no other income.

The reason for this is because you can utilise your annual, tax-free personal allowance.

In simple terms, the further your income is from the higher-rate tax bands, the more you will save in income tax by having the property in your sole name. This is especially true if your partner is a higher-rate taxpayer.

The following two case studies illustrate these points.

Sole Trader With No Income

Joanne is a married woman but does not work. Her husband is a high-flying executive who earns £70,000 per annum.

Upon the death of a relative, Joanne is left £100,000. She uses the entirety of this inheritance to purchase an investment property.

She makes £600 rental profit per month. (She bought the property with cash, so therefore she has no outstanding mortgage or other costs in the 2016-17 tax year).

This means that she makes an annual rental profit of £7,200.

She is not liable to pay any tax on this amount as it is within the annual personal income tax allowance of £11,000.

Had Joanne bought the property in joint ownership with her husband, then he would have been liable to pay tax at 40% on his share of the investment. If his share of the property was 50%, then he would have an annual tax liability of £1,440.

This means that over a 10-year period, Joanne will see a minimum tax saving of £14,400 by owning the property in her sole name.

Property Investor With No Income, but Partner Works

Chris is married and earns £15,000 per annum as a store sales assistant. His wife is a runs a pharmacy and earns £45,000 per annum.

They decide that they want to start investing in property and purchase a property for £45,000.

They take tax advice before investing and are told that they will pay less annual income tax if the property is purchased in Chris's sole name.

This is because he is not a higher-rate taxpayer.

5.3. When is it NOT Tax Efficient to Buy Property as a Sole Trader?

Try not to buy property as a sole trader if you are a higher-rate taxpayer i.e. paying tax at 40%, 45% or even 60%, especially if you can invest with a partner who is a lower-rate taxpayer.

If you are a higher-rate taxpayer, then you will have to pay income tax on any rental income at the higher rate as well.

It would be very poor tax planning on your end if you ended up paying 40%, 45% or 60% tax on all rental income, especially if you had a partner who could make use of the nil rate band or the 20% tax band.

5.4.   A Note about Selling Properties When Operating as a Sole Trader

You now know when it is beneficial to buy properties as a sole trader.

However, it is generally better to have a property in a joint name when you come to sell the property. The main exception to this rule is if the property has been your PPR; see section 25 for further details.

6. Income Tax & Property Partnerships

There is no doubt that owning properties in a partnership can be an excel'ent income tax–saving strategy.

In this section you will learn how owning properties in partnerships can significantly reduce your income tax bill.

6.1. What is a Property Partnership?

To put it simply, a property partnership exists when two or more people own a property in joint names.

When a property is held as a partnership, it is usually held in either of the following two ways.

6.1.1. Joint tenants

This method is most commonly used when a husband and wife purchase a property together.

The most important point about this method of ownership is that when one cf the joint tenants dies, the surviving tenant becomes the sole owner.

Owning Properties as Joint Tenants

Lisa and Alex are husband and wife and own a property as joint tenants. Unfortunately, Lisa passes away due to ill health.

The property now automatically becomes the sole ownership of Alex, without the need to wait for grant of probate or administration.

6.1.2. Tenants in common

This method is used when the owners of the property want to register the fact that they have separate ownership. This method is most commonly used when two or more unconnected people purchase a property together.

The most important point to note about this method is that when one of the 'tenants in common' dies, the property does not necessarily become the ownership of the surviving tenants.

> ### Owning Properties as 'Tenants in Common'
>
> Jack and Bill are two long-term friends who decide to start investing in properties together.
>
> They are also both married.
>
> Jack is the wealthier of the two, so when they decide to purchase a property, he funds 60% of the deposit. Therefore it is agreed that the property will be a 60:40 split in Jack's favour.
>
> They purchase the property as 'tenants in common,' where they specify that the property will be passed to their estate should either party die.
>
> Jack is the first to pass away. Upon his death, his 60% ownership in the property is passed to his wife.

6.2. When to Consider Buying in a Partnership

As we saw in section 5, you should generally try to avoid owning a property as a sole trader if you are a higher-rate taxpayer. This is purely because you will be liable to pay tax at the higher rate on any profitable rental income.

The two most important conditions that must be satisfied before investing with a partner are that

a) your partner must be a lower rate taxpayer than yourself; that is, if you pay tax at 40%. 45% or 60%, then your partner should pay tax at 20% or less;

b) you MUST be able to trust your partner(s).

> If you are already a nil-rate taxpayer, then don't go looking for a partner who is a higher-rate taxpayer.

This is because you will be unnecessarily passing on an income tax liability to your partner.

Instead, consider keeping the property in your sole name until your rental profits lead you to incur a tax liability at a rate that is equal to or greater than that of your partner.

6.3. Partners Must Be TRUSTWORTHY

If you buy property in a partnership, then you MUST make sure that the partners with whom you are purchasing are people who you **implicitly** trust, e.g., a spouse, your mother, your father, etc.

This is not just for tax reasons; it is simply good **BUSINESS PRACTICE**.

6.4. Partnerships between Husband and Wife

> HMRC will treat all properties purchased between husband and wife (other than shares in a close company) as a 50:50 split, unless otherwise stated.

In fact, HMRC treat all jointly owned property between husband and wife as an equal 50:50 split, unless otherwise stated.

This means that unless you tell HMRC otherwise, you will both be taxed 50:50 on any property rental profits.

A considerable amount of tax can be saved by having a property jointly owned by husband and wife, especially if one or the other is a nil- or a lower-rate taxpayer. It is important to note that if you intend to have a property between husband and wife as a non-50:50 split, then you must have an agreement between the two of you to say that this is the case.

It is not enough to just make a declaration to HMRC stating that a property is owned in unequal shares. It must actually be owned in this manner, and documentary evidence must be made available if requested by HMRC.

The following case study illustrates this scenario along with considerable tax savings.

Potential Tax Savings Between Husband and Wife

After five years of marital bliss, John and Lisa decide to buy an investment property.

John is a 40% tax payer, whereas Lisa is a homemaker and therefore has no income.

They buy a two-bedroom terraced house for £80,000. They decide to have the property as a 90:10 split between the two of them in favour of Lisa and produce documentary evidence to support this. They also inform HMRC of this split.

(The property is split in this manner to take advantage of Lisa's personal income tax allowance—in other words, they want to reduce their tax bill!)

They make £6,000 rental profit on the property on an annual basis. This means that the profit is split as follows:

- Lisa's share of the profit is £5,400;
- John's share of the profit is £600.

Lisa has no tax liability as her profit is within her tax allowance, and John pays £240 tax on his £600 profit.

If the property had remained as a 50:50 split, then the total joint tax liability would have been £1,200 (i.e. 40% of John's £3,000 share).

Therefore they have an annual savings of £960! Over 10 years, this gives tax savings of at least £9,600.

6.5. Partnerships between Those Other Than a Husband and Wife

If a property is purchased as a partnership between those other than a husband and wife, you **MUST** inform HMRC of the split.

In this type of partnership HMRC do not make any assumptions as to how the property is split. It is the taxpayer's duty to tell HMRC how the property has been split, and it must be based on fact.

For example, if you buy a property in a partnership with a friend, in which he or she provides 70% of the deposit and you provide 30% of the deposit, then you must also inform HMRC of the 70:30 split.

6.6. How to Declare a Partnership Split to HMRC

If you are a husband and wife wanting an unequal split, then you must make a declaration to HMRC about the ownership split.

Such a declaration takes effect from the date it is made, providing notice of the declaration is given to HMRC via Form 17 within 60 days.

If you would like to download a copy of Form 17, please visit the following link:

>> http://www.hmrc.gov.uk/forms/form17.pdf

It is important to note that the form only covers the assets listed on it. This means that if you have other properties that you want to be covered by the Form 17, they must also be listed to make HMRC aware of split.

Evidence of the ownership of the asset should also be provided to HMRC together with Form 17.

Please note that different HMRC offices differ with regards to what evidence is required to prove the ownership split for a property.

There are two common ways to prove the split.

   a) Provide a signed declaration by the two parties concerned detailing that ownership of the joint property is split in a specific way.

This is acceptable to some HMRC officers.

However, other officers will want more formal proof.

b) Provide more formal property documents that include the following:
   i. the deeds of conveyance;
   ii. bank accounts (to see letters to and from the bank confirming the change).

The best thing is just to send in (a), but be prepared to send in (b) if HMRC requires it or asks any further questions.

6.7. Moving Properties into Joint Ownership to Avoid Income Tax

If you have realised from this strategy that you can save tax by holding your property in a partnership, then you may well be thinking about how to transfer to joint ownership.

Well, it is actually very easy to do, and you will incur *no* capital gains tax liability if you are transferring part ownership to your spouse, i.e., your husband or wife.

PLEASE NOTE: If part ownership of the property is to be transferred to anybody other than your spouse, then there may be a capital gains tax liability triggered.

6.7.1. Three simple steps to follow

The following three steps will show you how you can transfer the property into joint ownership.

STEP 1. Contact your mortgage lender.

Tell your mortgage lender that you want to transfer the property into joint ownership, and explain why you want to do this.

Your mortgage lender will then send you a new mortgage application form for you to complete in order to move the property into joint ownership.

Unfortunately, lenders will treat transferring an existing property into joint ownership as though you are applying for a new mortgage. Therefore, it is very likely that you will have to submit the same paperwork again and effectively apply for a new mortgage.

It is likely that the property will be put into joint names on the same terms as the original contract; that is, if the original mortgage was fixed at 4.99% and had four years left to run on the fixed period, then the new mortgage will also be the same.

However, if mortgage rates have reduced, then be cheeky and ask if you can also have it at the new reduced interest rate!

STEP 2. Contact a solicitor.

Once your mortgage application has been approved, your solicitor can have all relevant documents changed into joint names pretty quickly. It usually takes about four weeks to complete all the legal paperwork.

Also, tell your solicitor whether you want the property to be owned as 'Joint tenants' or as 'Tenants in common', and how you want to split the ownership of the property. For example, you may want to hold the property in the majority of the lower rate tax payer, so that you pay less tax.

Whenever a property is being purchased by more than one person or transferred into multiple ownership your solicitor should always ask you how you wish to hold the property.

STEP 3. Notify HMRC.

If you decide to have an unequal ownership split, then tell HMRC of this split on the Form 17. The Form 17 must be submitted to HMRC within 60 days of the declaration.

Don't delay in notifying HMRC as it could well cost you in tax penalties.

6.7.2. Typical costs incurred when transferring

The costs that you are likely to incur when transferring the property will include the following:

- **Solicitor costs:** These are normally between £300 and £400. However, they will be less than the amount charged when buying a new house as searches will not need to be carried out again.

- **Mortgage lender fees:** The mortgage lender may or may not charge a fee for re-issuing the mortgage in joint names. Try hard to negotiate with them and see if they will waive it.

- **Stamp duty:** This may be payable dependent upon the mortgage amount that is being transferred. For example, if you are transferring more than £125,000 of the mortgage amount to your partner, then stamp duty will be payable at a minimum rate of 1%.

- **A valuation fee may also be incurred, especially if you are using the mortgage re-application** as an opportunity to release some equity from the property.

Please see section 20 to learn more about stamp duty.

It is important that you consider the tax savings you will make before you decide to transfer a property into joint names.

Ideally, you should calculate the cost of transferring the property into joint names and then consider how much income tax you will save on an annual basis.

The case study below demonstrates the importance of making such considerations.

Saving Tax When Moving a Property Into Joint Ownership

Alex has an investment property in his sole name and is a 40% taxpayer.

His wife, Lisa, is unemployed and has no intention of working.

Alex has an outstanding mortgage of £50,000 on the property, which is now worth £100,000.

He gifts 75% of the property to his wife and re-mortgages the property in joint names, with a 75:25 split in favour of his wife.

The cost of transferring into joint ownership is as follows:

- Solicitor costs   £500 approx.
- Mortgage lender fees   £variable
- Stamp duty   N/A. This is because 75% of the £50,000 mortgage is £37,500, and this amount is below the stamp duty threshold value.

He also calculates what the tax savings will be on an annual basis on a property income of £6,000.

Alex's tax liability   ➔ 40% on £1,500 = £600   (based on 25% ownership)
Lisa's tax liability   ➔ 0% on £4,500 = £0   (based on 75% ownership)

By having a 75:25 split, the combined tax liability is £600.

If Alex had kept the property in his sole ownership, then his tax liability would have been £2,400 (40% on £6,000 taxable property income) on an annual basis.

This means that both Alex and Lisa are making an annual income tax savings of £1,800.

7. How to Jointly Own a Property 50:50 but Split Rental Income 90:10!

This strategy has been written by Jennifer Adams.

An article in the *'Times'* stated that 53% of parents plan to financially support their offspring through university. Many will fund via savings, however, there is an alternative method of finance that should be considered.

This alternative method means that parents can subsidise their offspring and still keep their savings intact. There is also an added bonus of a minimal tax bill if correct procedures are followed.

7.1. What Has To Be Done?

- The parent(s) purchase a property (outright or via a mortgage) which is legally owned jointly with the student.
- The student resides in the property (rent free!) whilst undertaking their studies.
- The property is also let to other students who pay rent to the student as owner.
- The student uses the rent to finance his/her own personal expenditure

7.2. How Does This Work In Practice?

Many assume that when a property is owned on a joint basis any rental income received is also taxed in accordance with the same percentage proportion of ownership. For example, where a property is owned 50:50 then the assumption is that the rent must be taxed using the same 50:50 proportion.

However, this is not necessarily the case. The rent could be shared in varying proportions calculated to produce the maximum tax advantage for each owner, especially if one owner is a higher rate tax payer and the other a non or basic rate taxpayer.

Example
The purchase deed of 54 Dorchester Place, Oxford, shows that the property is owned jointly by John and his daughter Jane in the proportion 90:10. John is a 45% taxpayer, while Jane is a student and as such is a non-taxpayer. The net rental income for the year is £7,000.

Normally this would mean a tax bill of £2,835 for John on a 90% share of the income taxed at 45% whereas Jane would have no tax liability as the amount allocated to her is 10% i.e. £700 (which is covered by Jane's personal allowance).

On these figures, Jane will have to find another source of income to pay for her university living expenses unless Jack can subsidise her out of his already taxed income. The use of this proportion is therefore neither tax nor cash efficient.

It would therefore be more beneficial for the 90:10 split to be in Jane's favour. This would give Jane an income of £6,300 – below her personal tax limit of £11,000. The balance of £700 would be allocated to John to be taxed at 45% producing a tax bill of just £315.

John would still have £385 (i.e. £700 - £315), which is just enough to pay for any minor property repairs. The result of using this allocation is a tax saving of £2,520 per year and most importantly cash income – tax free - for Jane of £6,300 per year (a massive £18,900 over the three years that she is at university).

7.3. What Does HMRC Think of This Arrangement?

HMRC do not appear to mind at all! To quote from section 1030 of their 'Property Income Manual' under the heading 'Jointly owned property – no partnership':

"joint owners can agree a different division of profits and losses and so occasionally the share of profits or losses will be different from the share in the property. The share for tax purposes must be the same as actually agreed."

It would, however, be advisable to draw up a formal agreement in case HMRC require confirmation of the allocation. If written correctly, this agreement could accommodate any change in the owners' individual circumstances and the personal allowance amount on an annual basis.

The agreement should preferably be reviewed before the beginning of each tax year to record the allocation to apply for the coming year. An additional point (should HMRC query the allocation) is to ensure that the rental monies are paid in the correct proportions into each individual's bank account, reflecting the agreed share of income.

Importantly, the agreement will have no effect on the allocation of Capital Gains should the property be sold at a later date. Any taxable chargeable gain arising would be divided based on the actual ownership share as per the purchase deed; in the example given above, 90% would be charged to John and 10% to Jane.

7.4. Property Owners Who Are Married Couples

Married couples or civil partners who own property in joint names are automatically taxed using a 50:50 allocation. Therefore, this tax planning exercise only works if the property owners are unmarried. However, married couples can still take advantage of this tax saving scheme by changing the underlying ownership of the property to a different proportion, and using the Form 17 to inform HMRC.

7.5. Getting it Right!

The tax saving plan detailed above is clearly beneficial from an income tax point of view, however, care must be taken when the property is sold. Regardless of how the rental income is treated for income tax purposes it is the underlying beneficial ownership that determines the Capital Gains Tax treatment.

Therefore, the allocation must ensure that the full Capital Gains Tax allowance can be used by each owner. This may not be the case for a married couple who had chosen a 90:10 split, therefore the Declaration would need to be revised preferably a few months prior to the actual sale of the property enabling time for the required changes to be recorded by HMRC.

The plan is only available for adults over the age of 18 as the personal allowance cannot be used against income that comes directly or indirectly from a parent.

If other students shared the property with the owner, a claim for 'Rent a Room' relief could be made for income tax and, so long as the property remained Jane's 'Principal Private Residence', on disposal the property would be exempt from CGT. This would allow the personal allowance to be used against any other income.

Declarations of Trust should be limited to confirmation of the beneficial interest of each owner; any indication as to who should receive the share on death should be stated in a will drawn up by a solicitor.

8. Offsetting Interest Charges Before 6th April 2017

In this section you will learn about the different types of interest repayments that property investors may come across.

More importantly, you will understand when each of these types of interest can and cannot be offset against your rental income for the 2016-2017 tax year.

The rules for mortgage interest will be changing from 6th April 2017, and these are detailed in section 9.

8.1. Interest on Mortgages

It is probably fair to say that this is the most common type of interest that is associated with property investors.

This interest relates to the amount you pay back to your mortgage lender that is above and beyond the initial amount that you borrowed.

> It does not matter if the mortgage is a 'repayment' or an 'interest only' mortgage. The fact that interest repayments have been made means that they can be offset.

This is illustrated through the following case study.

Interest on Mortgages

John buys an investment property for £100,000.

The finance for the property is made up from a £20,000 deposit (provided from his personal savings) and an £80,000 buy-to-let mortgage (provided by a High Street Bank).

In the first year of the mortgage he pays £2,500 in mortgage interest. This entire amount can be offset against his income from the property.

This means that if he received £5,500 income from his property, he would only be liable to pay tax on £3,000.

8.2. A Note About 'Interest Only' and 'Repayment Mortgages'

As mentioned in the above tax tip, you are able to claim interest relief regardless of whether you have an 'interest only' mortgage or a 'repayment' mortgage.

8.2.1. Interest only mortgage

With an **interest only** mortgage you do actually only pay the interest that is charged on the amount that has been borrowed. The actual amount i.e. the capital amount remains the same and is usually due in one lump sum at the end of the mortgage term.

Interest Only Mortgage

Louise buys a property for £125,000 where her mortgage lender provides £100,000 on an interest only mortgage over 25 years.

Her monthly interest repayment is £500. She is able to offset the entire amount against the rental income.

However at the end of the mortgage term, she will still owe the £100,000 that has been borrowed.

8.2.2. Repayment mortgage

With a **repayment** mortgage you pay both the interest and the capital amount on a monthly basis. However you are only able to offset the amount that has been charged in interest. You cannot offset the capital repayments.

Repayment Mortgage

Same scenario as in the previous example. However this time Louise goes for a repayment mortgage of £100,000.

This means that her monthly repayments will be higher because she is repaying both the interest and part of the capital amount borrowed.

She makes monthly repayments of £650, where £400 is the interest repayment and £250 is capital repayment.

She is only able to offset the interest part of the repayment i.e. the £400. She is not able to offset the capital element of the repayment mortgage.

8.3. Interest on Personal Loans

If you take out a personal loan that is used 'wholly and exclusively' for the purpose of the property, then the interest charged on this loan can also be offset.

The important point to note here is that personal loans *must* be used in connection with the property.

Following are some typical property investment scenarios detailing when the interest charged on a personal loan *can* be offset against the property income.

8.3.1. *Loan used for providing deposit*

Most buy-to-let mortgage lenders require you to provide a 20% deposit before they will lend you the remaining 80% in the form of a mortgage.

If you don't have the 20% deposit, then it is likely that you may well need to finance the deposit by getting a personal loan.

If you do take out a personal loan for the 20% deposit, the interest charged on this loan can be offset against the property income.

If you are considering doing this, or have already done this, then what this means is that you have a 100% financed investment property, where interest charged on both the mortgage and the personal loan can be offset against the rental income.

Interest on Personal Loan Used For Deposit

Ali is desperate to buy his first investment property after seeing his pension fund plummet and his house value almost double within 5 years.

Unfortunately, (due to his lavish lifestyle), he has no savings of his own but is in a well-paid job, earning £40,000 per annum.

He sees an investment property advertised for £100,000, but his mortgage lender requests a deposit of £15,000.

He sources this deposit by acquiring a personal loan at a rate of 9% per annum.

The bank then agrees to finance the remaining £85,000.

This means that Ali has a 100% financed investment property. Therefore he is able to offset the interest charged on both his loan and the BTL mortgage against his rental income.

8.3.2. *Loan used for refurbishments/developments*

Periodically, you will need to refurbish or even develop a property.

Imagine that you have just purchased a property that needs totally re-decorating and modernising. If you take out a loan for this kind of work, then the interest charged on the loan can be offset against the property income.

Alternatively, you might decide to embark on a more expensive property extension, e.g., to build a conservatory.

Again, the same rule applies here: The interest charged on the loan can be offset.

Interest on Personal Loan Used for a Refurbishment

Karen buys an investment property for £100,000. She manages to pay the 15% deposit from her own personal savings and the remaining finance is acquired on a BTL mortgage.

Before letting out the property she decides that a new bathroom suite will greatly increase the chances of the property getting let quickly. She prices a replacement bathroom suite at £2,000.

Unfortunately she has already stretched her personal savings account by funding the deposit for the property.

Therefore she applies for, and is successful, in obtaining a £2,000 personal loan at an interest rate of 10%.

Because the personal loan is used to replace the bathroom suite in the investment property she is able to offset the entire interest charged on the loan against her rental income.

8.3.3. Loans used for purchasing products

If you purchase goods from retailers where finance is available and these goods are used in your property, then the interest charged can also be offset.

This is more likely to happen if you are providing a fully furnished property, e.g., a luxury apartment.

If this is the case, then you may decide to buy the more expensive items on finance.

Such items are likely to include

- sofas, dining table & chairs, beds;
- cooker, washing machine, fridge/freezer;
- carpets, flooring, etc.

If you are paying for these products over a period of time (e.g., 6, 12, or 18 months), then any interest charged by your creditor can be offset against your rental income.

Interest on Buy-Now-Pay-Later Loans

Continuing from the previous case study.

Once the bathroom suite has been replaced she decides that the property should be offered fully furnished.

She decides to buy some new kitchen furniture in a sale and buys it on a buy-now-pay later scheme where interest is charged at a rate of 27.9%.

Again she is able to offset the interest charged on the loan against the rental income.

8.3.4. Loans to continue the running of your business

There may be occasions when you need to borrow money because your need to pay some bills or employees but do not have sufficient funds in your account.

In such circumstances you may decide to apply for a short-term loan to make these payments. Again the interest charged on the loan can be offset against the property income.

Interest on Loan for Paying Bills & Employees

Alexander has a large portfolio of properties but has incurred a cash flow problem. This is because he has just paid for a major refurbishment on one of his properties by using funds in his property account, rather than acquiring some sort of finance.

This decision means that he is unable to pay his employees (who work in his property business) their end of month salaries and some property related utility bills that are due.

He applies for a short-term loan of £5,000 to make the necessary payments and interest is charged at 8%.

His is able to offset the interest charged against the income from his properties because it is incurred for the purpose of his property business.

8.3.5. Interest on overdrafts

If you have a separate bank account set-up for your property investment business then you may decide to apply for an overdraft rather than a personal loan.

If you decide to do this then as long as the overdraft is used for the purpose of the property business then you can offset the interest charged on the overdraft.

Interest Charged on Overdrafts

Using the previous example.

Instead of applying for a loan, Alexander decides to request a one-year overdraft limit on his account of £5,000. His application is successful and he is charged an interest rate of 7.5%.

Whenever he uses his overdraft facility and interest is charged, he is able to offset it against his rental income.

8.4. Interest on Re-Mortgages

If you have a mortgage on your investment property, then it is highly likely that you will consider moving to another lender at some point.

The main reason for this is because you will be trying hard to find a better mortgage deal!

As interest rates have been falling over the past few years, more and more people have been re-mortgaging their investment properties to capitalise on the better deals and to help grow their property portfolios.

Below are some pointers about re-mortgaging.

a) If you re-mortgage your outstanding mortgage with another lender, then you can *still* offset the interest repayments.

Interest on Re-Mortgages

Timothy has an outstanding mortgage balance of £50,000 on his investment property. He decides to move his mortgage from the Nat West to Lloyds as they are offering a lower rate of interest.

Timothy can still offset the entire interest charged by Lloyds on the £50,000 re-mortgage.

b) If you re-mortgage for a lower amount, then you can still offset the whole mortgage interest.

Re-mortgaging for a Different Value

Imagine the same scenario as in the previous example, where Timothy has an outstanding balance of £50,000 on his investment mortgage.

However, he inherits £20,000 from a family member, so he decides to use this toward lowering his mortgage liability.

Therefore he only re-mortgages to the value of £30,000 with Lloyds.

Again, the entire interest charged on the £30,000 can be offset against the property income.

c) If you re-mortgage for a greater amount, then generally speaking you can only offset the additional amount if it is used for the purpose of an investment property (however you may be able to exploit paragraph 45700 (see Understanding Paragraph 45700).

As property prices have sharply risen over the past few years, investors have been re-mortgaging their properties for higher values.

This is known as **releasing equity.**

If you have released equity or are considering doing this, then you need to follow the guidelines given above regarding the interest charged on personal loans.

You need to ask yourself,

'Is the additional equity release being used for the sole purpose of my property business?'

This can be illustrated through the following case study.

Releasing Equity

Timothy has an outstanding balance of £50,000 on his investment mortgage.

However, his property value has appreciated considerably, so he decides to re-mortgage with Lloyds for £80,000.

This means that he is releasing additional equity out of his current property to the value of £30,000.

He decides to use the equity release in the following way:

£20,000 is used to fund a new property investment, and it provides the deposit for his next buy-to-let investment. £10,000 is used to pay for a new car for his wife.

Now, Timothy can *only* offset the interest charged on both the outstanding mortgage balance of £50,000 and the £20,000 he is using as a deposit for his next purchase.

This is because this combined amount of £70,000 is used 'wholly and exclusively' for his property investments.

However, he *cannot* use the interest charged on £10,000 for buying the car as this cost is not associated with his property investments.

d) Generally speaking, because it is possible to obtain a lower rate of interest on your residential mortgage, more and more investors are deciding to increase the borrowing on their main residence and using this to reduce the investment mortgages.

Releasing Equity from Main Residence

Jack and Louise have a residential mortgage on their private residence for £100,000. The interest rate is fixed at 4.5%. They also have a BTL investment property. The outstanding mortgage on this property is also £100,000 but the interest rate is at a higher rate of 6.5%.

Because their main residence has a value of £300,000, they release £100,000 equity from their main residence, at the same rate of 4.5%, and pay off the outstanding debt of £100,000 on the investment property.

Again the interest charged on the £100,000 equity release can be offset against the rental income off the investment property.

8.5. Purchasing a Property with Cash and Then Re-mortgaging

Serious property investors are always looking for deals.

When one comes their way, it is sometimes not feasible to apply for finance. This is because the administration and paperwork will take too long, and this is likely to result in the investor losing out on the deal.

In such scenarios the investor will end up buying the property through their cash reserves, and they will then re-mortgage the property to release the invested funds.

The question then arises as to whether the interest charged on the re-mortgage is tax deductible.

In Arthur Weller's opinion, the mortgage interest is tax deductible in such scenarios. This is because the property was bought with the *intention* to take out the mortgage soon afterward.

In such scenarios the purchaser will only pay cash originally because this is a better way to execute the purchase.

Cash Purchase and Then Re-mortgaging

John has inherited £100,000 from his father's estate.

He is presented with the opportunity to purchase a property at £100,000, but he must complete the purchase within two weeks. By purchasing within two weeks, he will save £25,000 off the original asking price of £125,000.

John knows that it will take too long to apply for a BTL mortgage, so he pays for the property in cash.

Two months later, he re-mortgages the property using a standard BTL mortgage.

In this scenario, John can offset the interest on the re-mortgage as it was always his *intention* to fund the investment by a mortgage.

8.6. Understanding Paragraph 45700

Although we have generally stated that it is not possible to offset interest on a loan if it is not used for the purpose of the property, there is a ruling which is mentioned paragraph 45700 of HMRC Business Income Manual.

Paragraph 45700 gives landlords the opportunity to release equity from their investment properties and offset the interest regardless of what the equity release was used for.

The only restriction is that the equity release cannot be greater than the market value of the property when it is brought into the letting business. If the property had been originally bought for letting, this amount would be the purchase cost of the property.

In paragraph 45700, HMRC provides the following example:

'Mr A owns a flat in central London, which he bought ten years ago for £125,000. He has a mortgage of £80,000 on the property. He has been offered a job in Holland and is moving there to live and work. He intends to come back to the UK at some time. He decides to keep his flat and rent it out while he is away. His London flat now has a market value of £375,000. He renegotiates his mortgage on the flat to convert it to a buy to let mortgage and borrows a further £125,000. He withdraws the £125,000 which he then uses to buy a flat in Rotterdam.

HMRC go on to say that 'Although he has withdrawn capital from the business the interest on the mortgage loan is allowable in full because it is **funding the transfer of the property to the business at its open market value** at the time the business started. The capital account is not overdrawn'.

Here are some more case studies to explain the benefits of this tax break for landlords and homeowners.

8.6.1. *Benefiting from interest relief when buying off-plan*

Benefiting From Interest Relief When Buying Off-Plan

Alex buys an investment property off plan in January 2002 for £125,000. When the property is completed in June 2003 it is worth £175,000. Upon completion Alex decides to let the property and therefore the property is transferred to the lettings business at a value of £175,000.

This means that in the future years, Alex can remortgage the property for an additional £50,000 and still offset the interest that is charged. It does not matter what the £50,000 equity release is used for, it can be offset against the rental income, as the market value of the property at the time of letting was £175,000.

So if Alex wants to use the £50,000 equity to buy a new sports car then the interest charged on the equity release can be offset against the rental income.

It is important to understand that Alex is not allowed to offset any interest charges for equity that is released above £175,000 unless it is used for the purpose of the lettings business.

So this means that if in future years the property is valued at £300,000, then although he may be able to release additional equity above £175,000 he will not be able to offset interest on this amount if it used for anything other than the lettings business.

A tax efficient way to invest in property is to let out your existing residence and move into a new property (this is covered in further detail in section 0). This is because you will receive in particular two very generous tax saving reliefs:

- The '18 Month Rule' and
- Private Letting Relief

For more details about these rules, please go to section 0.

8.6.2. *Benefiting from Interest Relief When Letting Out Your Own Home*

Benefiting from Interest Relief When Letting Out Your Own Home

John and Louise buy a house in 1987 for £50,000. They live in it for 14 years and then decide to move to a bigger house. Instead of selling the existing house they decide to let it out.

Over the 14 years the house has been fully paid for and therefore there is no outstanding mortgage.

The value of the house in 2001 is £190,000. The new house that they have seen is £300,000.

In order to provide the deposit for the new house, they re-mortgage their existing house on a buy-to-let mortgage for £152,000. This amount is used to fund the deposit on the new residence, which means that they only need to borrow £148,000.

The entire interest that is charged on the buy-to-let mortgage can be offset against the rental income. This is because it is below the market value of the property at the time of letting.

Two years later the original property is worth £250,000. In order to reduce the mortgage on their private residence, they are able to release an additional £38,000 of equity on the buy-to-let mortgage. This means that they have mortgaged to the amount of £190,000 on this property.

Again, because they have not gone over the market value of the property at the time of letting they are able to offset the entire interest charges against the rental income.

At the same time they have also successfully managed to reduce the interest on their private residence by an additional £38,000!

Once again, if the original property is remortgaged above £190,000 and the money is not used for the purpose of the lettings business then the interest charged cannot be offset against the rental income.

9. Offsetting Interest Charges From 6th April 2017

This section has been written by Lee Sharpe.

9.1. Restricting Tax Relief On Mortgage Interest And Related Finance Costs

IN 2015 the Chancellor has announced that tax relief will be restricted for mortgage interest, etc., incurred for the letting of most types of residential property, or "dwelling houses", by individuals.

The restriction is not a complete disallowance but is likely to disadvantage many residential property landlords. In order to soften the blow, the disallowance is being introduced in stages over several tax years – "death by approximately four cuts", if you will.

Once fully implemented, this single measure is expected to cost landlords more than £660million in additional tax.

9.1.1. Will it Affect Me?

There is more than a good chance that many residential property landlords will be caught by the new rules.

Those who think they will be unaffected because they make only relatively small rental profits should consider carefully the effect of these changes as set out in the **Examples** below.

The new rules affect:
- Finance costs – interest, anything economically equivalent to interest, and incidental costs of obtaining finance, including to
  - Buy a dwelling to let out, or any interest in such a property and even to -
  - Develop land or existing property, to be let out as an ordinary dwelling(s), incurred in relation to -
- "Dwelling houses" – not defined in the legislation but most types of residential accommodation, including its gardens or grounds, by -
- Individuals – which will include individuals acting jointly (see also Partnerships, Companies and Trusts below)

Where the finance costs are incurred only partly for residential letting, then they are to be apportioned on a 'just and reasonable basis'.

When the measure was announced, the government said that it expected that roughly only 20% of individual landlords would be adversely affected.

I suspect that is nonsense. Given that HMRC also estimates that there are around 1.5million landlords in the UK, even this would represent a very large number.

However, the *real* number of landlords likely to be affected will probably be much higher, since the government appears to have factored in only taxpayers using "Buy-To-Let" ("BTL") mortgages. Most readers will be well aware that there are very many properties which are let out on normal mortgages – or at least not BTL mortgages – for various reasons.

Interest on any loan applied for a Furnished Holiday Letting business (or part of a larger letting business) will be unaffected by the new rules. Hotels are not property businesses from a tax perspective but trades, so will also be unaffected.

9.1.2. Partnerships, Companies and Trusts

The original guidance, which was published at the beginning of July, indicated that only individuals would be 'caught' by the new rules. Companies were not mentioned, nor were partnerships. The legislation itself, however, says **that interest will be disallowed for all property businesses subject to Income Tax.**

Individuals, partnerships and Trusts therefore seem all to be caught by the new rules. **Companies are specifically excluded**, except when acting in a fiduciary or representative capacity.

This means that non-Resident Company Landlords will generally escape the new restriction.

However, Trustees should note in particular that the provisions which give Basic Rate tax relief (see below) makes no mention of trusts.

9.1.3. How Will It Affect Me?

In effect, if you are a 40% or 45% taxpayer, then an extra £1 of tax relief from loan interest saves 40p or 45p respectively.

Restricting the tax relief to only 20% – 20p per £1 – means that this measure will effectively cost 20p or 25p in the £1 for Higher and Additional Rate taxpayers respectively.

The restriction will work by disallowing the finance costs entirely in the calculation of taxable rental profits (this part is being phased in over several tax years) and then separately *most** taxpayers will instead be able to claim Basic Rate tax relief of 20% on at least some of their disallowed interest costs. (A partner's share of the rental profits determines his or her share of the tax deduction).

There are, however, various restrictions to the 20% tax credit. This makes the calculation complex but the rationale appears to be that the tax credit is only used against 'full' 20% tax, rather than going against only 7.5% 'new' dividend tax, or savings which might be covered by the new so-called "Allowances" for savings and dividend income.

The adjustments appear to turn a blind eye to losses set against total income, however, which seems quite wasteful.

Most people will concentrate on the loss of Higher / Additional Rate tax relief, but disallowing finance costs and thereby increasing taxable rental income seems likely also to affect people on relatively modest incomes for:

- Student loan repayments

- Tax Credits entitlements

*The Income Tax deduction is available to individuals who are subject to Income Tax on an affected residential rental property business. This may prove problematic for Trusts which make discretionary payments of income to individual beneficiaries.

9.1.4. When Will It Affect Me?

The new rules will be phased in from April 2017:

- 2017/18   75% of finance costs allowable as in the past, and 25% gets only 20% tax relief
- 2018/19   50% of finance costs allowable as in the past, and 50% gets only 20% tax relief
- 2019/20   25% of finance costs allowable as in the past, and 75% gets only 20% tax relief
- 2020/21   No finance costs allowed against rental profits, 100% gets a maximum 20% tax relief

9.1.5. Examples Of New Interest Relief Tax Rules

1. Bill is an employed IT programmer and earns £50,000 a year. He is a 40% taxpayer.

He also lets out the property he used to live in, before he moved in with his spouse, and that property generates £5,000 a year net rental income after £3,000 interest deductions on an interest-only mortgage.

Tax Year:	2016/17 £	2017/18 £	2018/19 £	2019/20 £	2020/21 £
Earnings	50,000	50,000	50,000	50,000	50,000
Net Rent after Mortgage	5,000	5,000	5,000	5,000	5,000
Add-back Rental Finance	0	750	1,500	2,250	3,000
Total	55,000	55,750	56,500	57,250	58,000
Tax Liability Original	11,200	11,340	11,640	11,940	12,240
Rental 20% Tax Credit	0	-150	-300	-450	-600
Net Tax	11,200	11,190	11,340	11,490	11,640
Tax increase on 2016/17	0	-10	140	290	440

In the end, Bill is paying almost 50% tax on his rental profits, when all of his interest costs have been added back. The disallowance of loan interest relief at his main tax rate costs him far more in tax than the new 20% saving adjustment.

2. James is a full-time property investor, running 15 residential properties. He is heavily geared and his interest repayments eat up about 50% of his rent roll. Let's also assume that his interest costs of £40,000 a year increase by 5% per annum, as rates are expected soon to rise:

	2016/17 £	2017/18 £	2018/19 £	2019/20 £	2020/21 £
Net Rent after Mortgage	40,000	40,000	40,000	40,000	40,000
Add-back Rental Finance	0	10,500	22,050	34,728	48,620
Total	40,000	50,500	62,050	74,728	88,620
Tax Liability					
Original	5,800	9,240	13,860	18,931	24,487
Rental 20% Tax Credit	0	-2,100	-4,410	-6,946	-9,723
Net Tax	5,800	7,140	9,450	11,985	14,764
Tax increase on 2016/17	0	1,340	3,650	6,185	8,964

This example shows why landlords cannot ignore these new rules, even if they currently pay only 20% tax. Critically, the mortgage interest disallowance is enough to make James a 40% Higher Rate taxpayer anyway, because his interest costs are so high.

By 2020/21, James' *taxable* profits are more than double his actual profits because by this point his interest costs are fully disallowed.

9.1.6. What Should I Do?

This might seem like an open invitation to incorporate your property business – and in fact incorporation can offer numerous benefits, depending on the circumstances – but, as many readers will know:

- Companies generally find it harder to secure finance for BTL property
- Interest rates are usually significantly higher for corporate loans
- There may be significant "one-off" costs to incorporating an existing business, such as legal fees, Stamp Duty Land Tax and Capital Gains Tax, although Incorporation Relief may be available, thanks to the **EM Ramsay** case
- In terms of running your own company, dividend income is about to get a lot more expensive (see next Budget development)

If you have both a trade and a residential property business, then it would make sense to ensure that any finance costs are incurred more in respect of the fully deductible trading activity than the residential property business.

Taxpayers and advisers may well want to re-acquaint themselves with the guidance on tax relief on funding capital introduced into a business, in HMRC's Business Income Manual at BIM45700.

A similar approach might benefit those with both commercial and residential properties but 'partitioning' interest costs may be more difficult.

HMRC may well try to argue that, if the rental business is an aggregation for tax purposes, the interest should be apportioned rather than specifically allocated to commercial lettings which escape the disallowance. It is sometimes possible to own property in different capacities so that the net incomes are not aggregated but care and advice will be essential, with an eye in particular to the potential loss of flexibility of rental losses.

Will some landlords ditch residential property completely in favour of commercial letting? I suspect it will increase the appeal of commercials.

9.1.7. Why is the Government Doing This?

The Finance Bill Explanatory Notes argued that this measure would "...ensure that landlords with higher incomes no longer receive the most generous tax treatment."

Which is clearly nonsense, since those landlords with higher incomes will enjoy those higher incomes precisely because they have relatively fewer (or lesser) costs and by implication, lower interest repayments. It appears instead to be a politically astute revenue-raising exercise.

10. 10% Wear and Tear Allowance

In this section you will learn about a very important method that can be used to reduce your income tax bill.

Unfortunately, this was removed from 6th April 2016, but if you are completing tax returns prior to this date then the allowance can still be claimed for.

This is a relatively simple strategy to understand, and it relates to the furnishings provided in a property.

10.1. What is the 10% Wear and Tear Allowance?

The 10% Wear and Tear Allowance is an allowance that HMRC have introduced to make the lives of property investors easier when they complete their tax returns.

In a nutshell, it allows you to offset 10% of your annual rental income against your property income tax bill.

This sounds straightforward, and in principle, it is. However, there are some important points to note.

a) HMRC state that

   'The Wear and Tear Allowance is calculated by taking 10 percent of the next rental received for the furnished residential accommodation. To find the 'net rent' you deduct charges and services that would normally be borne by a tenant but are, in fact, borne by you (for example, council tax, water and sewerage rates etc.).'

   In most cases, it is very straightforward to calculate.

b) It does not matter how much you, as a landlord, spend on furnishing your property. You can only offset 10% of your net rental income.

c) The allowance can be used from the day that your property becomes furnished.

10.2. Understanding When the Allowance Can Be Used

> The 10% Wear and Tear Allowance can *only* be claimed when a property is **furnished** and before the 6th April 2016.

Before we go any further, it is worthwhile understanding what is meant by a **furnished** property.

Here is the HMRCs definition:

'A furnished property is one which is capable of normal occupation without the tenant having to provide their own beds, chairs, tables, sofas and other furnishings, cooker, etc.'

For a detailed explanation please visit:

>> www.hmrc.gov.uk/manuals/pimmanual/pim3200.htm

What this means is that a tenant can start living out of the property as soon as they move in. The only accessories that the tenant needs to provide are his/her own personal belongings.

More importantly, this means that the 10% Wear and Tear Allowance cannot be used for partly furnished or un-furnished properties.

Here are a couple of case studies to illustrate the use of this rule.

Simple Calculation of Wear and Tear Allowance

John rents out a fully furnished property.

He receives a monthly rent of £500.

The tenant is responsible for all property bills (i.e., utility bills) and services provided to the property (e.g., gardening).

The annual income for the property is therefore £6,000.

This means that John can offset £600 when he calculates his rental profits.

Complex Calculation of Wear and Tear Allowance

Imagine the same scenario as above, but this time, John is charging £600 monthly rent. He charges an extra £100 because John himself pays the utility bills and gardening services.

The annual income is now therefore £7,200.

John *cannot* offset 10% of £7,200 against his rental profits.

He first has to deduct the costs that would normally be borne by the tenant, which in this case is £100 per month.

Therefore he can only claim 10% on £6,000 (£7,200 – £1,200), which equates to £600.

10.3. Abolition Of The Wear And Tear Allowance

This section has been written by Lee Sharpe.

The guidance issued with the 2015 Summer Budget Statement announced that the Wear and Tear Allowance would be 'reformed' by replacing it with "a new relief" which would allow landlords to claim a deduction for the actual cost of replacing furnishings.

The guidance actually said:

"Currently, landlords of furnished properties can deduct 10% of their rent from their profit to account for wear and tear, irrespective of their expenditure. This means landlords can reduce their tax liability even when they have not improved the property."

It would perhaps be appropriate to point out:

- The Wear and Tear Allowance is available only to *fully* furnished properties
- It was never meant to encourage landlords to *improve* a property but simply to allow for the cost of maintaining its furnishings, etc.

It is also worth bearing in mind that the Wear and Tear Allowance was originally intended to cover items that a tenant or owner occupier would normally provide in unfurnished accommodation, e.g.:

- movable furniture or furnishings, such as beds or suites;
- TVs;
- fridges and freezers;
- carpets and floor-coverings;
- curtains;
- linen;
- crockery or cutlery;
- other white goods which, in unfurnished accommodation, a tenant would normally provide for himself (for example, cookers, washing machines, dishwashers).

In case any reader is experiencing a strong sense of déjà vu, the list is an almost verbatim lift from the venerable IR150 booklet – now deemed obsolete.

10.3.1. Will It Affect Me?

While the abolition of the Wear and Tear Allowance will affect only fully furnished residential properties, the "new relief" is likely to affect all residential properties, including those only partly furnished.

At the moment, HMRC's position is that the cost of replacing free-standing furnishings is not allowable, which is a deviation both from decades of former practice *and* their initial guidance published in December 2011.

Many tax advisers (including this one) disagree that the renewals basis, which (amongst other things) allows the cost of replacing free-standing furniture in a furnished property, was ever abolished by the withdrawal of either of the Extra-Statutory Concessions B1 or B47. Nevertheless, it seems likely that it will be less contentious to claim relief for such items, once the "new relief" is introduced.

10.3.2. How Will It Affect Me?

The following example illustrates the changes.

Example

Jennifer owns a flat which she lets out on a fully furnished basis, for £1,000 a month. As she owns much of the contents of the flat, she has a separate contents insurance policy which costs £500 annually. (As contents insurance would ordinarily be the tenant's burden an adjustment is required to the Wear and Tear Allowance claim).

In 2015/16, she replaces a television for £500. In 2016/17, she replaces the living room suite for £1,400.

	2015/16		2016/17	
	£	£	£	£
Gross Rent		12,000		12,000
Less:				
Replace TV/suite	N/A*		1,400	
Contents insurance	500		500	
Other costs	2,500		2,500	
		3,000		4,400
Net Rental Profit		9,000		7,600
Wear and Tear:				
Gross Rent	12,000		N/A	
Less:			N/A	
Contents Insurance	500			
			N/A	
	11,500		N/A	
Wear & Tear @ 10%	10%		N/A	
		1,150		0
Tax-Adjusted Profit		7,850		7,600

*As Jennifer is letting the flat fully furnished – i.e., it has been let with sufficient furniture for normal residential use – she is allowed to claim the Wear and Tear Allowance if she prefers. Where her actual costs are lower, then it clearly suits her to do so – but she cannot also claim the cost of replacing items which are 'covered' by the Allowance. (In fact, since April 2013, HMRC would say she cannot claim for the replacement of free-standing items anyway although, as mentioned above, that is a contentious issue).

Once the Wear and Tear Allowance is abolished from 6th April 2016 and effectively replaced by the new relief, it seems likely that free-standing items will become claimable again, as per the example above.

10.3.3. When Will It Affect Me?

The Wear and Tear Allowance is being abolished from April 2016 – the "new regime" should take effect from the same date.

10.3.4. Practical Points

The 10% Wear and Tear Allowance was intended to cover the costs of replacing furnishings, and not to benefit or to disadvantage claimants, although there might be some individual landlords who could derive a net benefit if the Allowance exceeded their annual costs of replacing furnishings.

The Wear and Tear Allowance was very simple to administer and, while a simple 'replacement basis' will also be a straight forward concept, it presents the following challenges:

- Recording and claiming the cost of all the many small items which will now have to be identified individually – cushions, spoons, cuddly toy, etc.
- Although some tenants will keep landlords informed as the tenancy progresses, it seems likely that there will be peaks of expenditure between tenancies – effectively when making good for a new tenant – compared to the relatively flat deductions previously enjoyed under the Wear and Tear Allowance
- This is in turn likely to exacerbate problems with finance costs as above, since the limited benefit of the replacement tax deduction is <u>broadly</u> restricted to no more than net rental profits for the year

The above example assumes that HMRC's statement that the new relief will "enable *all* landlords of residential property to only deduct costs they actually incur" can be taken at face value.

The new regime is unlikely to be called "the renewals basis". It may prove entertaining to cynical tax advisers to watch HMRC try to distinguish the new regime from the renewals basis which HMRC *says* it abolished in 2013.

11. 'Wholly and Exclusively'

This section will address the term 'wholly and exclusively.'

If you have ever read and tried to digest the Property Income Manual, then you will have noticed that this phrase is consistently mentioned in the guide.

By the time you have finished this section, you will know how to test if an expense satisfies this rule and whether it can be offset against your property rental income.

11.1. Understanding the Term 'Wholly and Exclusively'

> HMRC state,
>
> **'You can't deduct expenses unless they are incurred wholly and exclusively for business purposes.'**

To put it simply, this statement means that if you incurred an expense that was not used for the purpose of your property, in any way at all, then you cannot offset the cost.

Whenever you incur a cost for your investment property, always ask yourself,

'Has the cost been incurred wholly and exclusively for the property?'

If you can answer **YES** to this question, then it is highly likely you will be able to offset the cost against your property rental income.

11.2. What If Cost is Not Wholly and Exclusively Incurred for Property?

Sometimes you may incur a cost that is not used 'wholly and exclusively' for your property. However, a portion of the cost has been incurred for your property.

For such situations HMRC provide the following guideline:

'Where a definite part or proportion of an expense is wholly and exclusively incurred for the purposes of the business, you can deduct that part or proportion.'

What this effectively means is that you need to determine what part or proportion of the cost is attributed to your investment property. This is because you cannot offset the entire cost.

The following case study will help to illustrate this guideline.

Where Costs Are Not Wholly and Exclusively Incurred for Property

Bill has an investment property.

The bathroom is looking rather 'tired,' so he decides to re-tile it completely. He goes to a local tile shop, where they have an offer of 12 square metres of tiles for £240.

However, he only requires seven square metres for his investment property.

After some serious head scratching he appreciates that the deal is an excellent value for the money and too good to miss. He therefore purchases the tiles.

He decides to use the extra 5 square metres of tiles in his own house.

This means that the entire cost has not been incurred wholly and exclusively for the property. However, a portion of the cost, i.e., 7/12ths, has been incurred wholly and exclusively for the property.

He may therefore offset £140 (i.e., 7/12ths of £240) against his rental income.

11.3. Costs of Maintenance and Repairs

Once you have purchased and successfully let your property, any maintenance costs incurred that help prevent the property from deteriorating can be offset against your rental income.

It is very likely that at some point you will have to carry out some maintenance work to keep your property in an acceptable state of repair.

When this happens, you will be able to offset the cost against your property income as long as it satisfies the following condition.

- **It is not a capital improvement.**
  A capital improvement is when work is carried out that increases the value of the property.

Maintenance Cost
John is informed by his tenants that water is leaking from the upstairs bathroom into the downstairs living room.
He calls a plumber to repair the damaged bathroom water pipe and also hires a painter/decorator to redecorate the damaged ceiling.
The entire cost of the work is £300, and it can be offset against the rental income.

11.4. Typical Maintenance/Repair Costs

The following list details typical maintenance/repair costs that you are likely to incur and which you can offset against your rental income:

- repairing water/gas leaks, burst pipes, etc.;
- repairing electrical faults;
- fixing broken windows, doors, gutters, roof slates/tiles, etc.;
- repairing internal/external walls, roofs, floors, etc.;
- painting and redecorating the property;
- treating damp/rot;
- re-pointing, stone cleaning, etc.;
- hiring equipment to carry out necessary repair work;
- repairing existing fixtures and fittings which include:
  - radiators,
  - boilers,
  - water tanks,
  - bathroom suites,
  - electrical/gas appliances,
  - furniture, and furnishings, etc.

11.5. The Big Misconception About Costs When A Property Is First Let?

There is a common misconception among buy to let landlords – and some of their accountants – that the cost of repairs to a newly-purchased property cannot be claimed before it is first let out.

11.5.1. Allowable expenses

In fact, such repairs are an allowable expense provided certain conditions are met, and if allowable, they are treated as if they were incurred on the first day the property is occupied.

The important distinction is between work on the property which is "capital expenditure" - effectively, part of the cost of acquiring the property and making it fit for use in the letting business, and expenditure which is no more than routine maintenance – even if that maintenance is quite extensive as a result of the previous owner's neglect.

11.5.2. The test

The test is this: was the property fit to be let before the repairs were carried out? If it was, then the repairs are an allowable expense against the rent once the property is let.

The law on this subject is derived from two tax cases which were heard shortly after the end of the Second World War.

11.5.3. A cinema

In one case, Odeon Cinemas claimed the cost of repairs to various cinemas they had bought up after the end of the war and refurbished before opening them to the public again.

Although the cinemas in question were in a poor state of repair, the Court was satisfied that they were nevertheless usable, and Odeon were simply carrying out routine maintenance which had been neglected during the war. They were also satisfied that the price Odeon paid for the cinemas was not significantly lower as a result of the condition they were in.

11.5.4. A ship

The other case concerned a ship which was also bought just after the end of the war. It too was in a poor state of repair, to the extent that it was classified as not being seaworthy. Given the times, a temporary certificate of seaworthiness was granted on condition that the ship was sailed straight to a port where it could be extensively repaired.

When the claim for these repairs came to court, the verdict went against the ship-owners. This was because it was clear that (despite the temporary certificate granted because of the post-war shortage of ships) the ship was not fit for use and the repairs were necessary before it could be used for the owner's trade.

It was also the case that the price paid for the ship reflected the fact that it was unseaworthy. The cost of the repairs was therefore capital expenditure, being part of the cost of acquiring the ship as a useable asset for the trade, in contrast to the Odeon cinemas, which were already useable when purchased, and simply needed their neglected routine maintenance brought up to date.

11.5.5. Is your property a cinema or a ship?

This distinction between capital expenditure and repairs applies to any work carried out on a property, at any stage in its ownership, and there is nothing special about work carried out before the first letting. The same rules apply, and expenditure on normal maintenance is an allowable expense whether the property has already been let or it has only just been purchased.

That is why a landlord should look at the property he has just bought for his letting business and consider whether it is more like a rather tatty cinema, or an unseaworthy ship!

If you have difficulty persuading your accountant that this is the correct view, tell him to go to HM Revenue and Customs' website, and look at PIM2020 in their Property Income Manual under "Repairs etc. after a property is acquired".

11.6. Capital Improvements

If you carry out a capital improvement then you *cannot* offset this cost against your rental income.

This is because it is not classed as maintenance or repair work.

Capital Improvements

After years of owning his investment property, Fred applies for, and gets approval to add, a conservatory.

The cost of the conservatory is £20,000.

Because the conservatory has increased the value of the house by £30,000, it cannot be offset against the rental income.

Again, the cost will be offset against any capital gain that he makes when he sells the property.

REMEMBER: If you have made a capital improvement, then this cost can be claimed when you sell your property.

12. Replacing Your Fixtures and Fittings

This section will help you to understand what is meant by the term **fixtures and fittings** and when you can offset the replacement of them against your income tax.

12.1. What are Fixtures and Fittings?

These are items that are classed as being an integral part of the property. If a new tenant moves into a property, then they will expect these items to be in the property.

Examples of fixtures and fittings include

- windows, doors, light fittings;
- kitchen units;
- bathroom suites;
- gas central heating systems and radiators or hot water supply tanks;
- gas fires, etc.

The most important point to understand about fixtures and fittings is that any cost incurred in repairing them or replacing them with a like-for-like product can be offset against the property rental income. This is regardless of whether the property is un-furnished, partly furnished, or fully furnished.

For the remainder of this section we will focus on the replacement of fixtures and fittings.

Two important conditions must be satisfied before you can offset the cost of replacing fixtures and fittings. These are the following.

a) The cost must be a 'replacement' cost. In other words, it cannot be for the installation of fixtures and fittings that were not previously in the property.

b) The cost must be for a similar, like-for-like product.

If both these conditions are met, then the cost can be deducted from the rental profits.

12.2. Replacing Fixtures and Fittings

Whenever you decide to replace existing fixtures and fittings, they are likely to fall into one of the following three categories:

a) like-for-like replacement;
b) like-for-like replacement but with capital improvements;
c) replacement with superior fixtures and fittings.

Each of the above scenarios is treated differently when it comes to calculating your income tax bill, and each is illustrated in the following sections.

12.2.1. Like-for-like replacement

If you replace existing fixtures and fittings with similar like-for-like products, then the entire cost can be offset against the income tax bill.

Replacing With Like-for-Like (1)

Alex has been renting out his buy-to-let property for seven years and decides that it is now time to change the bathroom suite.

He finds a similar bathroom suite of comparable quality that costs £500. The cost of having the old suite removed and the new one fitted is also £500.

This means that the entire project costs £1,000.

This whole amount can be offset against the annual rental income.

12.2.2. What if it is not possible to replace with like-for-like?

HMRC appreciate that it is not possible to replace with a like-for-like product in all instances. This is especially true if you are replacing something that is several years old as a like-for-like product may no longer be available.

In such circumstances, it is possible to replace with a superior item, especially if it is of a similar cost.

Replacing With Like-for-Like (2)

Alex also decides to replace the wooden, single-glazed windows as they are starting to rot. The windows are more than 10 years old.

The cost of replacing with similar single-glazed windows is £3,500, and this includes the fitting and removal of the old, rotten windows.

However, the cost of replacing the windows with UPVC double-glazed windows is actually cheaper and costs £3,400. This price also includes the fitting and removal of the old windows.

Although the UPVC double-glazed windows are of a superior quality, HMRC accept that these types of windows are the 'standard' in all new build properties.

Therefore it is possible to use these as replacements and offset the entire cost incurred.

12.2.3. Like-for-like replacement but with capital improvements

If you replace the existing fixtures and fittings with a like-for-like product but also make a capital improvement, then you can only offset the cost of the like-for-like replacement.

Replacing With Like-for-Like but with Capital Improvement

Alex also decides to replace the kitchen units.

The cost of replacing the kitchen units with like-for-like replacements is £1,600. However, he has some additional space that he wishes to utilise, so he orders an additional three units at a cost of £600.

Alex is able to offset the cost of the £1,600 like-for-like replacement against his rental income.

However, the additional three units are treated as a capital improvement, and this cost cannot be offset against the rental income.

Instead, the cost of the additional units can be offset against any capital gain arising when the property is sold.

12.2.4. Replacement with superior fixture and fittings

If you replace the existing fixtures and fittings with superior fixture and fittings then it will be treated as a capital improvement.

13. Other Ways to Reduce Your Income Tax Bill

In the strategies to date you have learned about the common costs that can be offset against the rental income.

In this section you will now become familiar with numerous other typical costs that a property investor is likely to incur and that can be offset against the rental income.

13.1. Rents, Rates, and Insurance

The following costs are incurred by property investors when the property is let or when the property is empty and between lets.

13.1.1. Rents

The most common type of rent that an investor is likely to incur is ground rent. Landlords are liable to pay this rent on any leasehold property/land, and therefore any such expenditure can be offset against the rental income.

13.1.2. Rates

If you decide to pay any of the following rates on your property, then they can be offset against the rental income:

- water;
- electricity;
- gas;
- council tax;
- service charges;
- TV licence;
- telephone line rental;
- satellite TV charges, etc.

13.1.3. Insurance

Any insurance premiums that you pay for your properties or products/services relating to your property can also be offset against the rental income.

The most common premiums you are likely to pay will include the following:

- building insurance;
- contents insurance;
- insurance cover for service supplies such as
  - gas central heating,
  - plumbing insurance,
  - electrical insurance;
- insurance cover for appliances such as
  - washer/dryer,
  - fridge/freezer,
  - television, etc.

13.2. Can I Offset Pre-Trading Expenditure?

This is a bit of a grey area as far as taxation goes.

The rules for pre-trading expenditure are quite complex, but in theory you can claim expenses incurred in the seven years before commencement of the rental 'business.

The expenses are treated as incurred on the first day the rental 'business' starts.

Having said that, HMRC will want to examine these expenses closely with a view to establishing whether they were incurred 'wholly and exclusively' for the purposes of the 'trade.'

Again in theory HMRC can disallow any expense which has a duality of purpose, but in practice they will usually allow a split to be made.

They will also examine the expenses to see whether they are capital or revenue in nature.

Below is a list of some common types of pre-trading expenditure you are likely to incur before you buy your property:

- travel costs
- the cost of purchasing dedicated trade/magazines for helping you to find your property;
- the cost of telephone calls when phoning estate agents/property vendors, etc.

The important point to note is that each occurrence of a pre-trading expenditure must be incurred wholly and exclusively for the property.

13.3. Carrying Over Rental Losses

> Any rental losses made on a property can be carried forward into the next financial year.

Sometimes you will incur a rental loss on your property investment. Rental losses can be incurred intentionally or unintentionally. The important point to note is that any losses can be carried forward into the next year and can be used to reduce your tax liability for that year.

Carrying Over Rental Losses

After three years of owning his two-bedroom buy-to-let property, John decides to replace the bathroom suite. The cost of replacing it with a like-for-like replacement is £2,500.

His rental income for the property is £4,800 annually, but after all his annual expenses are deducted, e.g., offsetting interest payments, the cost of the replacement bathroom suite, etc., he is left with a £1,000 rental loss.

> This loss can be carried forward and offset against his rental income the
> following year.

13.4. Claiming Travel Costs

Below is an explanation of travel costs by Jennifer Adams.

A rented property portfolio may not be placed in the same street or even the same town as your main residence or place of work. Travel from one property to another, as the landlord dealing with problems as they arise, does cost. That cost is allowed as an expense against rental income received.

The treatment of travel expenses is similar to that as incurred by a trade or profession, such that to be allowed two key conditions need to be met:

- The expense must be related to the property in that it satisfies the '***wholly and exclusively'*** test; and

- It must not be incurred as a capital improvement such that the value of the property is increased.

13.4.1. 'Wholly and exclusively'

Confirmation that profits of a property are calculated using the same rules as for the computation of trading income is to be found in the tax legislation at s 272 of the *Income Tax (Trading and Other Income Act) 2005* (ITTOIA 2005) and hence the '***wholly and exclusively'*** rule applies such that there must not be duality of purpose of the expense incurred.

13.4.2. Office based at home

It is a question of fact as to whether the landlord carries on the rental business from his home. If so, the cost of all trips from home (e.g. to check on the investment property/liaise with tenants etc.) are fully allowable, provided that the visit is not also combined with a personal reason.

However, a deduction would still be possible for a journey where any personal benefit is incidental (i.e. '*de minimis*'); for example, the trip is made to the rental property but the landlord stops on the way to pick up a newspaper.

Furthermore, when making a claim for travelling expenses between the home base and a let property the real reason for the trip may need to be considered carefully.

For example, a landlord lets his main residence in Woking whilst working away from home in Brighton. He has travelled to Woking with his family to visit relatives at Christmas. Whilst in the area he may decide to drop by the rented property for a visit - this will be deemed a 'duality of purpose' visit, not fulfilling the 'wholly and exclusively' rules and hence the cost of travel will be disallowed for tax purposes.

Similarly, if the owner lives in London and has both a holiday home and a letting property based a few miles away from each other in Dorset, the cost of travel would only be allowed if the trip was made straight from the London base to the letting property without stopping at the holiday home first.

However, it would be fair to claim mileage from the holiday home to the let property.

13.4.3. Office outside of home

If the property business is *managed* from an office outside of the home then HMRC deems the business not to be carried on at home, even if the property owner sometimes works from home. In this situation the cost of journeys between home and either the property let or that office base will not be allowable.

However, the cost of travel from the office to and from the properties, and also between properties, will be allowable provided that the trip is incurred '***wholly and exclusively***' for rental business purposes.

13.4.4. Use of a letting agent

Some landlords engage a letting agent to manage the collection of rents, organise services etc. Where such an agent carries out all (or virtually all) the duties relating to the letting activity, it is likely that the rental business is being conducted through the agent.

In such circumstances, the business 'base' is deemed to be the agent's office and as such travelling expenses from the landlords' home to the property are not allowable but will be from the agents office to the property.

13.4.5. Relevant tax cases

Under the tax legislation (ITTOIA 2005, s 272) these cases are now relevant to a rental business:

- **Newsom v Robertson [1952]** - a barrister frequently worked from home but his chambers were separate. As such he was deemed not to be carrying on his profession from home and travel between home and chambers was not ***wholly and exclusively*** incurred for the purposes of his profession.

- **Horton v Young [1971]** - it was found that the claimant did carry on his trade from home and as such travel from home to the various sites at which he worked was undertaken for the purposes of the trade and claimable.

13.4.6. How much to claim?

- **Capital expenditure**
If the landlord uses his own car for travel, the full capital purchase cost of the car is not allowable; rather a proportion is, as capital allowances, claimed in the proportion of business use.

The '***wholly and exclusively***' rule also applies to that amount claimed and as with car running expenses only the business proportion is allowed. Allowances on cars costing in excess of £12,000 are further restricted. For detailed guidance see www.hmrc.gov.uk/manuals/pimmanual/PIM2210.htm and PIM3000 onwards, and HMRC's Capital Allowances manual.

- **Running expenses**

There are two methods of calculation for car expenses incurred - the same as for other business expenses.

1. A fixed rate for each mile travelled on business using HMRC's fixed mileage rates. Currently the first 10,000 business miles in relation to the rental business are claimed at 45p and 25p thereafter. This method of calculation is only available where certain conditions are met.

2. On an actual basis, such that the actual expenses (fuel, repairs, insurance etc.) are totalled and apportioned between business and private percentage using detailed records. For example, if a landlord agrees with HMRC that 70% of mileage incurred relates to expenses for the property business a 70% deduction is claimed (the same percentage is used for the capital allowance claim). Provided that the landlord proposes a percentage to add back/disallow which reasonably reflects the private element, HMRC will usually accept.

13.4.7. Misc. travel costs

If the trip to visit the property requires an overnight stay then hotel costs and meals in restaurants can be claimed; if public transport is used then the claim is the cost of the ticket.

13.4.8. Foreign travel

- If a foreign property is rented out then similar to any other business travel costs, car parking, hotel expenses, petrol, toll charges, flight costs etc. can be claimed providing that you can prove no 'duality of purpose' (e.g. that you did not visit the property whilst also on holiday)
- Incidentally, all foreign property rentals are treated as one business. Hence a claim can be made for the cost of travel to Dubai to look for a possible new rental property against the rental income from a villa already owned in Spain.

13.4.9. Expenses when not available for letting

Expenses incurred during any period whilst the property is *'not available for letting'*, are not deductible for tax purposes. This not only means that travel costs cannot be claimed but it also results in restrictions being made on other expenses that would otherwise be claimed including the mortgage interest.

13.5. General Property Costs

If you have a portfolio and incur expenses then it may not be possible to attribute the cost to a single property. This is because the expenditure may have been for all of the properties.

A good example of this is when purchasing decorating materials for a property. In such circumstances you can either:

- apportion the cost against the properties, or
- have a separate listing of generic expenses to add on at the end when you combine all the incomes and expenditures.

Either way is fine, as it makes no difference to the tax position, though practically the latter option may be easier and simpler to implement.

13.6. Storage Costs

A cost incurred by an increasing number of investors is storage costs.

The cost of renting storage space is allowable against rental income. The reason is that it fulfils the principal criteria of "wholly and exclusively", as the cost was incurred for the purpose of your property business. If you never had rented property then you would not be incurring such costs.

Storage Costs

John owns 5 properties which are all fully furnished. However he finds a new long-term tenant for his property who has his own furniture and furnishings. John decides that he will empty the property and store the furniture in rented storage. The cost of rental storage is £450. This amount can be offset against the rental income as it has been incurred 'wholly and exclusively' for the purpose of the rental business.

13.7. Other Common Landlord Expenditures

Below is a list of other common costs that a landlord will incur that can be offset against the rental income:

- safety certificates, e.g., gas and electrical safety;
- stationery, e.g., stamps, envelopes, books;
- computer equipment;
- bad debts;
- legal and professional costs, e.g., accountancy costs;
- service costs, e.g., window cleaner, gardener;
- furniture/appliance rentals;
- advertisement costs;
- letting agent costs;
- books, magazines, etc.;
- security/smoke alarms;
- telephone calls, including mobile telephone bills (but make sure you have an itemised bill to prove the calls made);
- bank charges (e.g., interest charged on property bank account).

13.8. Can I Offset the Cost of a Property Seminar?

During the property investment boom a large number of potential and inexperienced investors attended seminars and paid thousands of pounds for learning about various property investment techniques.

A common question that arises is whether the cost of the seminar can be offset against any future income tax bill.

When asked the question **'Can I offset the cost of a £5,000 property seminar?'** Arthur Weller provides the following guidance:

If the cost of the seminar is wholly and exclusively for the purposes of the trade presently carried out by the taxpayer, then it is allowable.

Here is what HMRC have to say about the matter:

> *'Expenditure on training courses attended by the proprietor of a business with the purpose of up-dating his or her skills and professional expertise is normally revenue expenditure, which is deductible from profits of the business provided it is incurred wholly and exclusively for the purposes of the trade or profession carried on by the individual at the time the training is undertaken'.*

So what exactly does that mean?

Already a property investor
If you are already a property investor, with a portfolio, and attend the course to update your investment skills, then you can offset the entire cost.

You can offset the cost as you will be regarded as updating your skills.

When You CAN Offset the Cost of a £5,000 Property Course

Bill has been investing in property since the early 1980s and has built a portfolio of 12 properties.

However, in 1999 he decides take property investment more seriously and attends a £5,000 course to update and sharpen his investment skills so that he can focus on emerging areas for investment.

The entire cost of the course can be offset against his rental income.

New to property investment
However, if you want to start investing in property and attend a course to learn how to do this, then you will not be able to offset the costs against the rental income.

You cannot offset the cost as you will not be 'updating' your skills in your current profession.

When You CANNOT Offset the Cost of a £5,000 Property Course

Following the collapse of the stock market, John decides that the only way he will be able to maintain his lifestyle when he retires is if he invests in property.

So, in 2001 he attends a property investment course to learn all about property investment. Shortly after the course he buys his first investment property. The cost of the course cannot be offset against any future rental income.

<u>A word of warning</u>
If you do decide to make a claim, it could well trigger an investigation. HMRC do keep a close eye on large amounts being claimed, so be warned!

13.9. Capital Allowances for Landlords

If you decide to purchase a piece of equipment or an asset that is used for the purpose of the business then you can claim an 18% annual depreciation allowance. Examples of such assets include:

- Computers and office furniture (that you use in your own home for running the business)
- Tools for maintaining upkeep of properties i.e. DIY tools
- Vehicles (please note that there are new rules for claiming capital allowances on vehicles for expenditure incurred from April 09 onwards).

The depreciation allowance can be claimed annually until the equipment/asset is disposed of. Here is an example that shows how the 18% / 20% depreciation allowance works.

Capital Allowances for Assets

Wasim has a portfolio of five investment properties. He also carries out much of the maintenance and repairs on the properties himself, so he decides to purchase professional DIY toolkit for £150 in April 2008. The annual depreciation allowance is calculated as follows:

Tax Year	Toolkit Value	Annual Rate	Annual Allowance
2008-2009	£150	20%	£30
2009-2010	£120	20%	£24
2010-2011	£96	20%	£19.20
2011-2012	£76.80	20%	£15.36
2012-2013	£61.44	18%	£11.06
2013-2014	£50.38	18%	£9.07

As you can see from the above example, the amount that can be claimed on an annual basis continues to decrease as the toolkit value decreases.

---

14. Running Your Property Business From Home

Sarah Bradford considers how tax relief can be obtained for the fixed costs of running a business from home.

Many small businesses are run from home and a proportion of the costs of running and maintaining the home can be deducted in computing the profits of the business.

Broadly speaking, expenses fall into two categories – fixed costs and running costs. Fixed costs are those that have to be incurred regardless of the level of trade. Costs that relate to the house as a whole will generally fall into this category. Running costs (or variable costs) are costs that vary depending on the extent of use, such as electricity.

This strategy looks at how relief may be obtained for the fixed cost and at example of typical fixed costs in respect of which relief may be available.

14.1. Nature of Relief

Where a business is run from home and part of the home is set aside solely for business use for a specific period, a proportion of the fixed costs incurred in relation to the home will be allowed as a deduction in computing the business profits. It will generally be necessary to apportion the fixed costs between the business and non-business element. A reasonable basis of apportionment would be one which reflects the proportion of the house used for solely business purposes and the time for which it is so used.

Using an area of the house solely for business purposes can have capital gains tax consequences, as the main residence exemption does not apply to any part of the property used for business use. Where only a small part of the house is used solely for business, in most cases the availability of the annual exemption means this is rarely a problem in practice, as any chargeable gain arising is normally covered by the annual exemption. However, to be on the safe side it is sensible to set aside the room used for the business for sole business use during working hours to preserve the deduction for fixed costs but to make it available to the family in evenings and at weekends to keep it within the main residence exemption.

14.2. Typical Fixed Costs

Costs which may be incurred in relation to a house or other property and which are classified as fixed costs include:

- buildings and contents insurance;
- council tax;
- mortgage interest;
- rent; and
- repairs and maintenance.

Each of these is discussed in more detail below.

14.3. Insurance

Depending on the nature of the policy, insurance can be either a fixed or a variable cost. Buildings insurance will generally cover the whole property, and where a business is operated from home a deduction can be obtained for a proportion of the premium.

As regards contents insurance, if contents are covered as part of a general buildings and contents policy, a proportion of the total premium can be deducted; likewise in relation to a separate contents policy that covers all household contents and does not exclude business items. However, if there is a specific trade policy, the premiums for that will be deductible in full, but there will be no deduction in relation to the domestic policy.

14.4. Council Tax

The extent to which a deduction is permitted in respect of council tax will depend on the circumstances. Council tax is a property-based tax payable on chargeable dwellings. By contrast, business rates are charged on commercial property. Depending on the size and scale of the business and the degree to which the premises are used for business purposes, the council may charge business rates.

However, where a trader merely sets aside a room in his or her home as an office, it is likely that only a council tax charge will apply. Where this is the case, the trader can claim a proportion of the council tax as a deduction in computing the profits of his or her business.

14.5. Mortgage Costs

Where the house is subject to a mortgage, a deduction may be permissible in respect of a portion of the mortgage costs. However, where the mortgage is a repayment mortgage it is necessary to split the payments into the capital repayment element and the interest element. Repayments of capital are not deductible, whereas a deduction is allowed in respect of the interest element and the trader can claim a portion of the interest element of a mortgage as a deduction in computing profits.

14.6. Rent

Where the trader rents his or her home and runs a business from a home office, a deduction is also available in computing profit if part of the home is used solely for business purposes. The allowable amount is the proportion of the rent payable to the landlord that is attributable to that part of the home used solely for business purposes.

It should be noted that where the business is run as a limited company, the homeowner can charge rent to his or her company in respect of the part of the home used by the company. The rent paid is deductible by the company in computing the profits for corporation tax purposes, and the homeowner is taxed on the rent that he or she receives. By contrast, where the business is operated by a sole trader, the homeowner cannot charge the business rent.

14.7. Repairs and Maintenance

All buildings will need some general maintenance at some point. Where part of the home is used solely for business purposes, a deduction is permitted for a proportion of general household repairs and maintenance to the extent that they apply to the property generally, rather than to a specific room. Examples of repairs and maintenance costs which may be apportioned include roof repairs and painting the exterior of a property. However, where the repairs or maintenance relate solely to a part of the room which is not used for business purposes, no deduction is permitted. By contrast, repairs or maintenance that relate wholly to the part that is used for business purposes are deductible in full.

It should be noted that no relief is available in respect of capital expenditure and a distinction is drawn between a repair (for which a deduction may be allowed) and improvements which are capital in nature and not deductible in computing profits. As a general rule, a repair restores something to its original condition, whereas an improvement significantly enhances it.

Practical Tip
It is easy to overlook the fixed costs of running a home when computing business profits, but it can be worthwhile claiming a deduction where part of the home is used exclusively for business. An additional deduction is available for running costs, which can be claimed either by reference to the actual costs incurred or by using the statutory simplified expenses deduction.

15. Tenant Deposits: Traps & Tips

15.1. Deposits from Tenants

This strategy has been written by Sarah Bradford.

It is common practice for a landlord to take a deposit from a tenant when letting a property to cover the cost of any damage caused to the property by the tenant. A deposit of this nature may be referred to as a security deposit, a damage deposit or a rental deposit. The landlord may also ask for a holding deposit in return for taking the property off the market while the necessary paperwork is undertaken.

15.2. Security Deposits

It is normal practice for landlords to take a security deposit from tenants when letting residential property. The purpose of the deposit is to cover items such as damage to the property that extends beyond normal wear and tear, the cost of having the property, including the carpets, professionally cleaned, removing any rubbish from the property, unpaid rent and such like. The items covered by the security deposit should be stated in the letting agreement.

The deposit charged can be up to two months' rent, although in practice six weeks' rent is common.

Deposits taken by a landlord or agent for an assured shorthold tenancy in England or Wales are protected by Government authorised schemes. There are three possible schemes:

- the Deposit Protection Service scheme;
- the Tenancy Deposits Solution scheme; and
- The Dispute Service scheme.

To remove the need to go to court to settle disputes over retention and repayment of the deposit, each scheme features an alternative dispute resolution service. In the event that there is a dispute regarding the repayment of the deposit in the case of damage or unpaid rent, the alternative dispute resolution service will arbitrate.

The burden of proof falls on the landlord or agent, who will need to provide evidence to support their claim that all or part of the deposit should be retained. If there is no dispute, the tenant's deposit should be returned to the tenant at the end of the tenancy.

The extent to which the deposit is included as income of the rental business depends on whether all or part of the deposit is retained by the landlord. In a straightforward case where a security deposit is taken by the landlord, held for the period of the tenancy and returned to the tenant at the end of the rental period, the deposit is not included as income of the property rental business.

However, if at the end of the tenancy agreement the landlord retains all or part of the deposit to cover damage to the property, cleaning costs or other similar expenses, the amount retained is included as income of the property rental business.

The retained deposit is a receipt of the business in the same way as rent received from the tenant. However, the actual costs incurred by the landlord in making good the damage or having the property professionally cleaned are deducted in computing the profits of the business.

The retained deposit is reflected as rental income of the property rental business for the period in which the decision to retain the deposit is taken, rather than for the period in which the deposit was initially collected from the tenant.

Example
Bill purchases a property as a buy to let investment. He lets the property out in September 2009. He collects a security deposit of £1,000 from the tenant. The terms of the deposit are set out in the tenancy agreement.

The let comes to an end in September 2011. When checking out the tenant, it transpires that the tenant has failed to have the carpets professionally cleaned, as per the terms of the agreement, and also that he has damaged a door, which needs to be repaired.

After discussion, Bill and the tenant agree that Bill will retain £250 of the deposit to cover cleaning and repair costs. The balance of the despot (£750) is returned to the tenant in October 2011.

Bill spends £180 having the carpets professionally cleaned and £75 having the door repaired.

Bill prepares accounts for the property rental business to 31 March each year.

When preparing accounts for the year to 31 March 2012, Bill must include as income the £250 retained from the tenant. However, he can deduct the actual cost of cleaning the property (£180) and repairing the door (£75). As the amount actually spent (£255) exceeds the amount retained, he is given relief for the additional £5 in computing the profits of his property rental business.

The balance of the deposit returned to the tenant is not taken into account as income of the business.

As stated in the article on use of the property rental toolkit in our September issue, HMRC recognise that accounting for deposits can sometimes cause problems. Guidance on income that should be taken into account in computing the profits of a property rental business can be found in their Property Income Manual at PIM1051 (see www.hmrc.gov.uk/manuals/pimmanual/PIM1051.htm).

15.3. Holding Deposit

Holding deposits are another form of deposit commonly taken by landlords, particularly in periods where the letting market is buoyant and demand for property is high. As the name suggests, a holding deposit is paid by the tenant to secure the property while the tenancy agreement is signed. In return, the landlord will take the property off the market.

A holding deposit is usually in the region of one week's rent. The terms governing the use of the deposit and the circumstances in which it may be retained by the landlord should be set out in a holding deposit agreement so all parties know where they stand.

In the event that the let falls through and under the terms of the agreement the landlord retains some or all of the deposit as compensation for the inconvenience and costs incurred in relation to the prospective let, the amount of the retained deposit should be included as income of the property rental business. However, the landlord would be able to claim a deduction for any costs actually incurred in relation to aborted let, such as advertising or legal fees.

In the event that the let goes ahead, the holding deposit would either be returned to the tenant or used to form part of the security deposit (see above). If the holding deposit is returned, it does not form part of the income of the business. Where the holding deposit is used as part of the security deposit, as explained above, it is only taken into account to the extent that it is retained by the landlord to cover damage etc. at the end of the let.

Practical Tip
As a general rule, deposits taken from tenants only form part of the income of the property rental business to the extent that the deposit is ultimately retained by the landlord. Any deposits that are merely held on the tenant's behalf before being returned to the tenant are not taken into account as income. On the other side of the coin, a deduction is given for any costs actually incurred by the landlord in making good damage etc. covered under the terms of the deposit agreement.

15.4. Tax Treatment Of 'Gifted Deposits'?

A recent case before the First-tier Tribunal (Day and Anor v Revenue & Customs [2015] UKFTT 142 (TC)) holds some valuable lessons for landlords selling a buy-to-let property.

One of the properties in the above case had been sold using a 'gifted deposit' scheme.

15.4.1. Gifted deposit schemes

These schemes used to be very popular and were promoted as a way of becoming a property owner without having to come up with any of the purchase price. The seller of the property would agree to take (say) 5% less than the asking price (which was itself often a somewhat inflated one), but this would be done by the seller making a 'gift' to the buyer of the 5% difference. The buyer could then obtain a 95% mortgage on the stated purchase price, but the other 5% was provided by the seller so the buyer had none of their own money invested in the property.

Everyone seemed quite relaxed about this practice, even though to me it looked very much like a fraud on the lender of the money, if they were not informed about the 'gift'. I recall raising this with a senior manager at one of the high street banks and asking what he thought about it. He asked me one question: 'In this hypothetical situation, does the buyer keep up with the mortgage payments?' When I replied 'yes', he gave me his professional opinion: 'Why should I care, then?'

This particular scheme was operated in the above case with the full knowledge of the lender involved – indeed the scheme was organised by the Halifax. Under the scheme, Mr Day and his co-investor effectively paid the 5% deposit on the sale to themselves, purportedly on behalf of the buyers, and the Halifax provided the buyers with a loan of the other 95% of the sale price. The point was to enable the Halifax to lend the buyers the whole of the actual purchase price whilst being able to record it as a 95% mortgage rather than a 100% one.

15.4.2. Tax treatment

HMRC contended that the sale proceeds for capital gains tax (CGT) purposes should be the whole amount shown in the sale documentation (£66,300), rather than the price after the 'gifted deposit' of £62,985.

The Tribunal described the £66,300 as 'a label' and agreed that the correct sale proceeds were the amount after the gifted deposit - £62,985.

The important point, however, was what they said about gifted deposits in general and their view of the rights and wrongs of them. In the Day case, the gifted deposit had been paid with the full knowledge (indeed, with the encouragement) of the Halifax, the lender concerned. The Tribunal suggested their view might have been very different if the deposit had been 'gifted' without the lender's knowledge (as many were when this was a popular ruse in the buy-to-let market).

They did not mince their words, either:

"If the appellants had fraudulently paid the deposit in order to help the purchasers obtain a 95% mortgage, we might well not have been persuaded that the appellants could rely on that fraud to reduce their tax liability."

The thing that saved Mr Day and his co-investor was that this was one of the 'respectable' gifted deposits, because the lender concerned knew about it and indeed was promoting it. Things might have been very different if it had been one of the 'under the counter' schemes that were around at the time.

15.4.3. Practical Tip :

If you bought a property using a gifted deposit scheme, the correct purchase price for CGT purposes when you come to sell it is likely to be the price net of the gifted deposit.

If anyone suggests using a gifted deposit, make certain the lender is fully aware of what is going on, and agrees to it.

16. The Two Ways to Calculate your UK Property Rental Income Profits

Most landlords are unaware that there are two methods that can be used to calculate your annual UK property income tax. These methods are known as **'Cash Basis'** and **'Earnings Basis'**.

In this article we will explain when and how both methods can be used.

To demonstrate each of the methods the following case study will be used:

Louise owns one buy-to-let property, which generates an annual rental income of £12,000. The rent is paid six months in advance and runs from 1st January 2013 till 31st December 2013. She starts to rent it out on 1st January 2013.

This means that she receives £6,000 in rental income on 1st January 2013, £6,000 on 1st July 2013, and £6,000 on 1st January 2014. The 1st January 2013 rental income covers the period 1st January to 30th June the 1st July 2013 rental income covers 1st July 2013 to 31st December 2013, and the 1st January 2014 rental income covers 1st January 2014 to 30th June 2014.

She also has some roof repairs carried out in the property in March 2013. The cost for the work done is £1,000. However the builder is a little slow in billing and he does not raise the invoice till May 2013 which Louise promptly pays.

16.1. Cash Basis

The cash basis can be used when the income generated from your property rental business (before allowable expenses are deducted) does not exceed £15,000 in the tax year.

When the cash basis is used, the income tax calculation is based on when the rent was actually **received** and when expenditures were **paid**. Note here that the emphasis in this method is on **'received'** and **'Paid'**. In other words it is based on when money exchanges hands.

Louise completes her tax return using the 'Cash Basis' method
When she completes her tax return the rental income will attributed to the tax years as follows:

Rental Income Received
2012-2013 tax year rental income is £6,000. This is because the first payment of 1st January 2013 lies in this tax year.

2013-2014 tax year rental income is £12,000. This is because the two payments of 1st July 2013 and 1st January 2014 lie in this tax year.

Expenditure Incurred
The roof repair work was carried out in the 2012-2013 tax year, as it was carried out in March 2013. However the invoice was not paid till the following tax year. This means that Louise will only be able to offset the expenditure against the 2013-2014 tax year as this is when the invoice was paid i.e. May 2013. Her net rental income for 2013-

2014, the amount she is taxable on, will be £11,000, i.e. £12,000 income less £1,000 expenses.

16.2. Comments about the Cash Basis Method

HMRG give the following in their manuals:

We are, therefore, prepared to accept the use of a 'cash basis' (profits based on the cash paid and received in the year) provided all the following conditions are met:

- the case is small; by a 'small' case we mean one where, for any year, the total gross receipts of your rental business (before allowable expenses are deducted) don't exceed £15,000; and

- the 'cash basis' is used consistently; and

- the result is reasonable overall and does not differ substantially from the strict 'earnings basis'

16.3. Earnings Basis

The earnings basis is also sometimes referred to as the 'accruals basis' and follows ordinary commercial accounting methods. When using this, method there are two very important points to note:

Firstly – You can use this method regardless of whether the income generated from your property rental business (before allowable expenses are deducted) exceeds £15,000 in the tax year. In other words if you annual rental income is below £15,000 per year then you can still use this method. However if it is above £15,000 then you must use this method.

Secondly - The income tax calculation is based on when the period the rental income **arises** and when expenditures were **incurred**. Note here that the emphasis in this method is on '**arises**' and '**incurred**' which is different to the cash basis method.

Let's continue with the case study:
Louise completes her tax return using the 'Earnings Basis' method
When she completes her tax return the rental income will attributed to the tax years as follows.

Rental Income Received
As we know, £6,000 was paid for the first six months that the tenant lived in the property. The upfront £6,000 payment on the 1st January 2013 was to cover the period 1st January to 30th June. However, this payment covered both the 2012-2013 and 2013-2014 tax years.

Therefore the £6,000 rental income needs to be apportioned across both tax years, as the rental income attributable from 1st January to 5th April will be recorded against the 2012-2013 tax year and the income attributable from 6th April to 30th June to the 2013-2014 tax year.

Here is how the apportionment could be done:

Daily Rental Income
£6,000 was due for 181 days (i.e. 1st Jan to 30th June).

This means that the amount charged per day = £6,000 / 181 = <u>£33.15</u>

Rental income for 2011-2012 tax year
The number of days from 1st January to 5th April inclusive = 95 days, and 95 * £33.15 = £3149.25.

Therefore <u>£3,149</u> is attributable to and recorded against the 2012-2013 tax year.

Rental income for 2012-2013 tax year
The remaining rental income from 6th April to 30th June is attributed to the 2013-2014 tax year. This amount is £2,850.75.

Also, the entire rental income of £6,000 that is paid on 1st July is also attributed to the 2013-2014 tax year. This is because it covers the period 1st July to 31st December.

This entire period sits within the 2013-2014 tax year. Also the rental income attributable to the period 1st January 2012 to 5 April 2014 is taxable in 2013-2014 tax year. This amount is £3,149.25. Therefore the total taxable rental income in 2013-2014 tax year is £ (2,850.75 + 6,000 + 3,149.25) = £12,000.

Expenditure Incurred
Even though the payment for the roof repair work made in May 2013, the work was actually carried out in March 2013. This means that because March falls within 2012-2013 tax year the £1,000 cost will be attributed to this tax year.

As you can see it is beneficial to offset the cost in this tax year rather than waiting till the following tax year.

Comments about the Earnings Basis

Here are some important points to note when using this method.

- This method must be used if your gross income exceeds £15,000 per tax year. However you can also decide to use it even if your income is less than £15,000.

- In the case study we calculated the amount due for the five odd days in April. HMRC do allow a concession here to simplify the computation. The concession allows you to ignore the split if you do it consistently across both income and expenditures and the figures are small. The strict daily apportionment is required when the figures are 'substantial'. Please note that there is no indication given by HMRC as to what is meant by 'substantial'.

- As you have seen here we are not working on the basis of what was **paid** or **received**. Therefore if a tenant did not actually pay the rental income that was due then you would create a bad debt to offset this against the rental income.

Companies and Property Taxes

17. Can a Limited Company Improve YOUR Tax Position?

In this section you will learn whether holding your properties through a company will benefit your tax position.

17.1. The Most Commonly Asked Tax Questions

'Should I buy my property through a limited company?'

'Should I move my properties into a limited company?'

'Is it true that I can save tax by holding my properties in a limited company?'

I am sure that, like most investors, you will have either asked or been involved in a discussion where these questions have been debated.

In all fairness, the answer to these kinds of questions depends on the following three key factors:

        a) your chosen investment strategy;
        b) your personal and financial circumstances/ambitions;
        c) how long you intend to hold on to the properties.

However, before you even decide whether a limited company will improve your tax position, there are some very basic rules and guidelines that must be understood.

17.2. Transferring Properties into a Limited Company

Do you already own investment properties?

Are you already on the buy-to-let investment ladder?

If the answer is yes, and you are now considering whether moving your properties into a limited company will save you tax, then consider the following FACT:

Properties must be transferred into a Limited Company at market value, unless a portfolio exists that is deemed to constitute a 'business'.

Yes, that's right!

Generally speaking, moving properties into a company is treated in the same way as if you were selling the properties.

If you bought your investment property ten years ago and you would now like to move it into a limited company, then you are likely to have to pay an *immediate* capital gains tax liability.

This is due to the fact that property prices have significantly increased over the past few years.

The exception to this rule is if the property is your **principle private residence**.

Transferring Properties into a Limited Company

Alex bought five investment properties, and their combined purchase value was £250,000.

Some years later they are worth a combined total of £550,000; that is, the combined value of his portfolio has more than doubled!

This means that his capital gain is £300,000.

By transferring the properties into a company, he may be liable to pay tax at both 18% and 28% on this amount, which means that he will have an immediate and significant tax liability (excluding any reliefs).

17.3. Don't Forget Stamp Duty!

Another 'tax bombshell' that may well hit when transferring properties into a ltd company could be stamp duty. Stamp duty land tax (SDLT) is charged on the market value of the properties being transferred into the company, even if gifted for no consideration, if the company is connected to the individual transferring the properties, which it usually is. If a number of properties are being transferred together, there is a new rule which says that the amount of SDLT charged is averaged out, as long as it is not less than 1%. Nevertheless SDLT will be payable.

> **Do not** start to form a limited company before you know what your tax liability will be.

17.4. Understanding 'Limited Liability'

There is a common misunderstanding by many property investors who believe that if they hold their properties in a limited company, they will escape from the banks/creditors if anything goes wrong.

As a separate legal entity, the company is, in theory, responsible for its own debts and liabilities. However, it is *very likely* that any lender will insist on a personal guarantee from the directors or shareholders when lending to the company. This means that if the company fails, the directors *will be liable*!

Consider the following case study.

When Limited Liability Will Not Help You

Mr and Mrs Prone form the limited company ABC Ltd. They borrow 75% of the purchase price and proceed to rent out the property through the company. They withdraw every penny of rent received without considering any tax consequences.

At the end of the first year the mortgage company decides to repossess the property as the mortgage has not been paid for six months.

In the above case study the directors will be held responsible for paying

- the outstanding mortgage;
- corporation tax on the profits;
- any tax due on the money that they have withdrawn.

This is because the liabilities have arisen as a direct result of their actions.

By law, directors are largely responsible for the actions of the company, and hence if it all goes wrong, there is a fair chance that the directors will find themselves personally liable for any debts arising as a result of their decisions.

However, having the cover of **limited liability** can still be useful if the business incurs unexpected (i.e., outside the control of the directors) losses or liabilities.

Such losses and liabilities can occur when

- a property development goes horribly wrong;
- tenants refuse to move out, and the company runs out of cash to pay the mortgage;
- interest rates suddenly double;
- the housing market crashes (let's hope this doesn't happen!);
- a tenant is injured on your property and successfully sues the company for personal injury.

This last pointer is a very good reason for ensuring that you have the correct landlord's insurance in place.

Let's look at another case study to illustrate the point.

Using Limited Liability to Your Advantage

Mr and Mrs Prone decide to enter the buy-to-let market and set up a limited company to hold the property. The property costs £100,000, and a loan is obtained from the bank for 85% of the purchase price.

Tenants are found and a rental agreement signed. No insurance is taken out as it is not considered a priority.

Three months later, a solicitor's letter arrives claiming that the tenant has fallen down the stairs as a result of improper maintenance of the stairways (there is a hole in one of the stairs).

After much debate and a court case, compensation is set at £150,000. The directors are cleared of any responsibility in the case by the judge. Clearly, the company cannot pay this amount of money, and the company is put into liquidation.

In the above case study the owners have been successful in that the limited liability of the company has saved them from being personally responsible for the costs.

If this had not been in place, then the costs would have fallen on them, which would have resulted in them having to sell their own houses to meet the claim.

17.5. Two Major Tax Benefits of Using a Limited Company

As a general rule, if you intend to re-invest the money you have made through your property investments, e.g., you want to continue re-investing the profits into acquiring more properties, then it will be beneficial to invest through a limited company.

There are two *significant* tax benefits of growing a property portfolio through a company. These are explained below.

a) Lower-rate tax savings.

As a higher-rate taxpayer, you pay 40% on your profit and gains. For a limited company the tax rates are, for the year beginning 1 April 2012, 20% for a small company, and 24% for a big company. This figure of 24% is being reduced to 23% for tax year beginning 1 April 2013, to 21% from 1 April 2014, and to 20% from April 2015. A small company is a standalone company (i.e. no associated companies – under common control) which has profits of £300,000 or less in a twelve month period.

b) Stamp duty savings.

You only pay stamp duty at a rate of 0.5% when purchasing company shares[1].

17.6. Other Benefits/Drawbacks of a Limited Company

17.6.1. Benefits

Here are some more favourable tax benefits to consider when deciding whether to own your properties through a limited company.

---

[1] This only applies when purchasing a company that already owns the property. It does not apply when a company purchases a property.

- A company can define its own accounting period that does not exceed 12 months.

- Indexation relief is still available for any capital gains.

- You will see lower tax rates as companies pay tax at 20%, going down to 19% from April 2017, going down to 17% from April 2020.

- Properties can be transferred within group companies without incurring a tax liability[2].

- You can grow a portfolio more quickly within a company by continuing to re-invest

- Dividends can be extracted from a company in a tax efficient way.

17.6.2. Drawbacks

Here are some drawbacks that you should consider before deciding to own your properties through a limited company.

- Companies cannot use the annual personal CGT allowance. £11,000 for 2014-15 and £11,100 for 2015-2016 and 2016-2017.

- Official company accounts must be produced. The cost of drawing up such accounts can be three to four times more expensive than having your sole trader accounts drawn up.

- Banks are less willing to lend money if you are purchasing through a company.

---

[2]This only applies in a group situation, e.g., a holding company with a 75% subsidiary or subsidiaries.

18. Incorporating A Property Business

This section has been written by Lee Sharpe.

18.1. Introducing The Incorporation Game

Many readers will be aware of new measures announced in the 2015 Summer Budget, which will phase in the disallowance of mortgage interest (and related finance costs) for residential property businesses over the next few years.

These measures apply only for Income Tax, and companies are specifically excluded from the measures (by and large, except where acting in a fiduciary or similar capacity). It seems likely that a substantial number of property investors will look to incorporation as a potential solution.

18.2. Warning!

There is far more to incorporating a business than trying to avoid a hefty tax rise. Companies are separate legal entities and, like the directors who run them, are bound by legislation, such as the Companies Act 2006.

The assets transferred to the company, and the profits it generates, belong principally to the company, and only indirectly to the shareholder(s) who owns the company. Tailored professional advice is absolutely essential when contemplating a transaction at this level.

18.3. Tax Considerations

There are numerous issues to consider on transferring a property investment business to a company, including:

1. Capital Gains Tax
2. Stamp Duty Land Tax
3. VAT – if there are any commercial properties
4. Capital Allowances

18.3.1. Capital Gains Tax (CGT)

A mature property investment business is likely to be worth much more than what it originally cost to acquire and develop. Many people assume – incorrectly – that there is no CGT to pay if you give assets away and no money changes hands.

Basically, CGT is due on the market value of an asset transferred by way of discount or outright gift, no less than if full consideration were received. There are exceptions, such as most transfers between spouses/civil partners, and gifts of underlined trading assets, but these are unlikely to be relevant to a property business.

In the absence of any reliefs, a CGT charge is in point, on transferring a property investment business into a limited company. Fortunately, a relatively recent tax case (*EM Ramsay* v **HMRC [2013] UKUT 0226**) found in the taxpayer's favour when she incorporated her business and claimed Incorporation Relief.

18.3.2. CGT Incorporation Relief

This relief applies to **postpone** the capital gain that arises when a person transfers chargeable assets into a company, in return for the issue of shares in that company. It is important to note that:

- It is essentially an "all or nothing" transfer: all of the business assets must be transferred into the company; one cannot pick and choose which assets are transferred.
- The relief applies to the extent that it is only shares which are issued in exchange for the property transferred; other consideration will result in at least part of the gain becoming taxable.

The net result of this relief is that the gain which would otherwise have been taxed on incorporation, becomes 'embedded' in the shares now held in the company, until they are sold or otherwise disposed of. Of course, if there is no intention to sell the shares, then the gain is postponed indefinitely.

One final important point about Incorporation Relief is that it is by no means certain that a property business will qualify for the relief. While the **Ramsay** case confirmed that a property business *may* qualify, it would be wrong to assume that all property businesses will qualify.

Critically, the taxpayer was able to demonstrate that she actively participated in running a property business. For many property investors, their activity is a full-time occupation; others may for instance delegate day-to-day running to a letting agent, which may prove problematic.

It may be possible to check with HMRC if they think that a particular property business is eligible or not. See HMRC's Capital Gains Manuals at CG65700.

18.3.3. Stamp Duty Land Tax (SDLT)

Generally, where a property is transferred as a gift, then it may avoid SDLT. Unfortunately, there are provisions in the SDLT regime which result in a charge based on market value, when property is transferred to a company under the control of the transferor. Having said that, there are also provisions which allow partners in a normal 'general' partnership (or a Limited Liability Partnership) to transfer property to a connected company without an SDLT charge.

While a partnership might at first seem to offer a relatively simple route to avoiding the potential SDLT charge on incorporation, a jointly-owned property investment business is, in the eyes of the taxman, no more a partnership than a jointly-held bank account. This is arguably quite unfair to joint owners who might actively work together to run a property business, but the legislation and HMRC's interpretation are quire unhelpful in this regard – see for instance the Property Income Manual at PIM1030.

Even so, it may be possible for jointly-owned rental businesses to demonstrate the degree of commercial organisation required in order to 'qualify' as a partnership. Limited Liability Partnerships have the potential to force the issue in favour of the taxpayer, although anti-avoidance legislation can be triggered where it seems to HMRC that a partnership (or LLP) has been created in order to avoid an SDLT charge, rather than for genuine commercial reasons.

Two final points about SDLT:

- It may be beneficial to claim Multiple Dwellings Relief, to derive an SDLT charge based on the 'average' market value.
- When transferring 6 or more properties, it may be advantageous to apply the "non-residential use" SDLT rates, which are capped at 5%, rather than the maximum 12% for residential properties in a lettings business.

18.3.4. VAT

Aside from short-term letting such as hotels and holiday lettings, renting out residential property is exempt from VAT, so the transfer to a limited company should not trigger a VAT charge.

Care is needed, however, where commercial property is transferred alongside; such a disposal may be subject to VAT, and there may also be implications for having Opted to Tax the property/ies, the business' Partial Exemption position and the Capital Goods Scheme may also be in point.

However, VAT may be avoided because a "Transfer of a Going Concern" is outside the scope of VAT. (Which will help reduce SDLT as well, since it is calculated inclusive of VAT).

Even if the incorporation does escape a VAT charge, a new registration / change of entity may have to be notified to HMRC.

Remember that if you want to claim CGT Incorporation Relief, you may have no choice but to transfer commercial property alongside residential – all of the business should be transferred.

18.3.5. Capital Allowances

This is again particularly relevant for commercial properties, where Allowances may have been claimed in the current business.

Incorporation will cease the original property business for the purposes of Capital Allowances, and by default a balancing event will arise, although it should normally be possible to make a joint election to transfer at the prevailing Written Down Value to avoid a charge.

It may in some cases be possible to reduce the proceeds even further and generate further tax allowances.

This will be particularly beneficial where the original owners are subject to 40% Income Tax, but the company will pay only 20% Corporation Tax; taking the relief before incorporation would save 40% rather than just 20% later on in the company.

It is also important to note that a joint election (and asset pooling where appropriate) will be required in order for the company – and any subsequent buyer – to be able to claim Capital Allowances on any fixtures in the property at the point of transfer.

18.3.6. Conclusion

There are numerous tax aspects to incorporating a business. It is also important to understand that it is not necessarily easy to *dis*incorporate, should the need arise later. As mentioned at the outset, tailored advice is essential.

19. How to Use a Property Management Company to Save Income Tax

The previous section gave an insight into the tax implications of owning your properties through a limited company.

In this section we have featured an article written by James Bailey (www.taxinsder.co.uk). In this article he considers whether it is still beneficial to use a property management company following the changes to the previous nil-rate tax band.

19.1. Will a Property Management Company Save Me Tax?

The article is titled: **Property Management Companies – Are They Still Going to Help Slash your Property Tax Bills?**

Consider the following case study:

Say you own half a dozen properties, which produce gross rents of £60,000 a year, and a rental profit of £40,000 after expenses. Depending on your circumstances, you will be paying income tax at 40% on at least part of this profit – let's say, on £10,000 of it. You set up a company to manage the rentals. It does not own the properties – it charges you a fee for managing them, in the same way any other letting agency or estate agent might.

A typical "arm's length" property management fee is between 10% and 15% of the rents received, so if we take 15%, the company will charge you £9,000 for collecting your £60,000 rents. It will probably cost about £600 per year to run the company (accountant's fees, etc.).

Is it still worth it if the company is paying Corporation Tax (CT) at 20%?

If you are a basic rate taxpayer, the answer is no – the basic rate of income tax is 20% and CT is 20%. If you pay tax at 40%, is it still worth considering?

On the figures we used above, you save £3,600 income tax (£9,000 at 40%). The company pays CT at 20% on its profits of £8,400 (£9,000 fees, less £600 running costs), so the CT due is £1,680. Taking the running costs into account, the saving is now £1,320 (income tax saved = £3,600, less CT due £1,680 and running costs £600).

If you want to get the money out of the company, you have a choice; you can pay yourself dividends, but as a higher rate taxpayer your effective rate of income tax on these will be 32.5% on any amount above the £5,000 dividend allowance. Looking at our company again, it will have cash of £6,720 after paying its expenses and its CT. If you pay that out as a dividend, £559 income tax will be due (£5,000 @ 0% plus £1,720 @ 32.5%).

If you liquidate the company after running it for at least one year, entrepreneurs' relief will mean that you pay capital gains tax @ 10%.

This all goes to show that although a property management company can still save you some money, it would be pretty borderline unless your rentals were approaching the £100,000 per year mark. Above those levels, however, it is still worth considering.

A word of warning – the strategy of liquidating a company to get the cash out free of tax is "provocative" (that is tax adviser's jargon for "it makes tax inspectors very cross") – you can't do it too often, and you **must** have advice from a tax specialist to avoid getting into trouble with the taxman! The Government are currently introducing new legislation to counteract 'phoenixism' - closing down a company, extracting the funds and paying a small amount of capital gains tax, and then starting a new company soon afterwards.

19.2. Draw Up Formal Contracts Between You and Your Company

> *Do not* set up a company that manages your properties and just simply start paying money into it.

If you just go ahead and start making payments into your company, then the Inland Revenue could challenge you (if you are ever investigated) for making artificial transactions to avoid paying tax.

If you find that by using a property management company you will improve your tax position, then it is advisable to draw up a simple contract between you and your company.

Just drawing up a simple contract that outlines the services your company is providing to you will help to prevent such a challenge!

19.3. Beware of Artificial Transactions!

Arthur Weller advises that you need to be careful and make sure that you are not creating artificial transactions that are aimed at avoiding tax.

In order words, the payments that you make to the company must be realistic and believable by the taxman.

For example, if you have a single property, then you can't pay £750 a month for property management–related charges. It is just not believable, and if you are ever investigated, then the taxman will for sure question whether you were making artificial transactions to avoid paying tax.

You must therefore pay an amount into a company that is believable and relates to the property. A good guide for you is to charge what a letting agent normally charges for their services. So, if your property management company charges you about 15% of your rental income, then this is both realistic and believable.

So, this means that

- for a rental income of £400pcm you can pay your company £60pcm;
- for rental income of £800pcm you can pay your company £120pcm;
- for rental income of £1,200pcm you can pay your company £180pcm.

Stamp Duty Land & Property Tax

20. Saving on Stamp Duty

In this section you will understand when you are liable to pay stamp duty.

20.1. When Do Property Investors Pay Stamp Duty?

The Chancellor of the Exchequer announced a change in the stamp duty rates during his 2015 autumn statement. The following table provides details of the current rates of stamp duty for residential property which have become effective from 1st April 2016.

A new series of stamp duty rates have been introduced for second and subsequent residential properties, which will be effective for property investors.

Stamp Duty Rates

	First residential property	Second and subsequent residential properties – from 1 April 2016
When payment for the property is up to £40,000	Zero	Zero
When payment for the property is over £40,000, then the SDLT on any amount up to the first £125,000	Zero	3%
Next £125,000 (£125,001 to £250,000)	2%	5%
Next £675,000 (£250,001 to £925,000)	5%	8%
Next £575,000 (£925001 to £1.5 million)	10%	13%
Remainder above £1.5m	12%	15%

The example that follow will assume that the second and subsequent residential properties stamp duty rate applies.

20.1.1. Stamp Duty when Buying New Land or Property

When purchasing land or property, you will be liable to pay stamp duty before you have completed the deal. Typically, the solicitor acting on your behalf in the transaction will include this tax liability in his final invoice to you.

Stamp Duty Land Tax When Buying A Second Property

Haleema buys a second property for £185,000.

The rates of stamp duty will be as follows:

The first £125,000   -   3%
The next £60,000   -   5%

The means the total amount payable will be:

The first £125,000   -   £3,750
The next £60,000   -   £3,000 (£60,000 * 0.05)

Total Due: £6,750

This means the total amount of stamp duty due is £6,750.

Stamp Duty When Purchasing A Second Property

Howard buys a buy-to-let property for £500,000.

The rates of stamp duty will be as follows:

The first £125,000   -   3%
The next £125,000   -   5%
The next £250,000   -   8%

The means the total amount payable will be:

The first £125,000   -   £3,750
The next £125,000   -   £6,250 (£125,000 * 0.05)
The next £250,000   -   £20,000 (£25,000 * 0.08)

Total Due: £30,000

This means the total amount of stamp duty due is £30,000.

20.1.2. *Stamp Duty when Transferring a Property*

What a lot of investors fail to realise is that if you transfer ownership of a property to another party (including husband/wife), then stamp duty will be liable if the property is mortgaged and the mortgage amount being transferred is over £40,000.

If the property is not mortgaged and ownership is being gifted, then there is no stamp duty liability.

Stamp Duty When Transferring A Second Property

This case study continues from the previous case study, where Howard has now purchased his property and already incurred a charge of £30,000 in stamp duty.

Two years after the purchase, he marries his long-term girlfriend Betty. He decides to move the property into joint names, where they will have equal 50:50 ownership of the property.

The outstanding amount on the mortgage at the time of transfer is £200,000. By transferring the mortgage into joint names, Betty will liable to pay any additional stamp duty tax as follows on her share of £100,000 of the mortgage:

The first £100,000   -   3%

The means the total amount payable will be:

The first £100,000   -   £3,000

                    Total Due: £3,000

This means the total amount of stamp duty due is £3,000.

Other Property Investment Strategies

21. Tax-Free Income for Renting Out Part of Your Home

In this section you will learn about generous annual tax-free savings that are available if you rent out part of your main home.

This tax relief is known as the **rent-a-room** relief.

21.1. What is the Rent-a-Room Relief?

If you decide to let a room in your main residence, you can receive a rental income of up to £7,500 and have no tax liability[3]. This new rate has become effective from 6th April 2016.

Prior to this the rate was £4,250.

In order to claim this allowance, the property must satisfy the following conditions:

a) you must also live in the property as your main home, at the same time as the tenant, for at least part of the letting period in each tax year;

b) the room you are letting out must be fully furnished.

If you claim the rent-a-room relief, then it is not possible to claim any expenditure that you have incurred with regards to the letting.

This is a very common strategy for those people who have houses that are too large for their needs. For example, if your children have left home, then you may decide to rent the room they lived in for an additional tax-free income.

Rent-a-Room Relief (1)

Bill and Mary have a three-bedroom detached house. They are both higher-rate taxpayers.

Their daughter Louise leaves home and moves in with her long-term boyfriend, so they decide to let her room out to a local teacher.

They receive an annual rental income of £4,000 per annum.

There is no tax liability on this income as it is below the £7,500 threshold value.

If the income received is greater than the annual allowance, then tax is liable on the amount above this value.

---

[3]All that is necessary is to tick the rent-a-room box at the beginning of the land and property page of the tax return.

Rent-a-Room Relief (2)

Howard is a bachelor but lives in a luxury five-bedroom detached house on the outskirts of London. He is also a higher-rate taxpayer.

He decides to let a room to a newly graduated doctor for £8,500 per annum.

Howard will have no tax liability on the first £7,500. However, he will be liable to pay tax on the remaining £1,000 of income at 40%. This means that he will be liable to pay £400 in tax.

If you decide to let a room in your main residence and claim the relief, then you must inform HMRC. This is regardless of whether you will have a tax liability.

If you do not inform HMRC, then you will be taxed as though you are running a normal property-letting business, where your expenses will be deducted from any rental income you receive.

21.2. Choosing Not to Use the Relief

Consider not using the relief if you have high income and also high expenses.

If you are letting a room in your property, then it is not necessary that you claim the relief. As mentioned in the previous section, you will be taxed as a normal property-letting business if you do not inform HMRC that you want to use the relief.

Generally speaking, if your rental income is going to be significantly greater than £7,500, then it may not be beneficial to use the relief.

The following two case studies illustrate typical scenarios when it is beneficial to use each method.

When it is Beneficial to Use the Rent-a-Room Relief

John is a higher-rate taxpayer and lets out a room in his property for £10,000 per annum. His expenses are £1,000.

Tax liability if rent-a-room relief is *not* claimed
If rent-a-room relief is not claimed, then he has a taxable income of £9,000 (i.e., £10,000 – £1,000).

This means that his tax liability is calculated as follows:
40% × £9,000 = **£3,600**

Tax liability if rent-a-room relief *is* claimed

If rent-a-room relief is claimed, then he has a taxable income of £2,500 (i.e., £10,000 − £7,500).

This means that his tax liability is calculated as follows:
    40% × £2,500 = **£1,000**

As you can see from the above case study, it is beneficial for John to claim the rent-a-room relief. This is because by claiming it, John will pay **£2,600** less in tax on an annual basis. Over a 10-year period, this is **£26,000** in tax savings.

When it is NOT Beneficial to Use the Rent-a-Room Relief

Lisa is a higher-rate taxpayer and lets out a room in her property for £13,000 per annum. Her expenses are £9,000 per annum.

Tax liability if rent-a-room relief is *not* claimed
If rent-a-room relief is not claimed, then she has a taxable income of £4,000 (i.e., £13,000 − £9,000).

This means that her tax liability is calculated as follows:
    40% × £4,000 = **£1,600**

Tax liability if rent-a-room relief *is* claimed
If rent-a-room relief is claimed, then she has a taxable income of £4,500 (i.e., £13,000 − £7,500).

This means that her tax liability is calculated as follows:
    40% × £5,500 = **£2,200**

As you can see from the above case study, it is beneficial for Lisa *not* to use the rent-a-room relief. This is because by claiming it, Lisa will pay **£600** less in tax on an annual basis. Over a 10-year period, this is **£6,000** in tax savings.

It is possible to switch between the 'Rent-a-Room' allowance and the "strict" method from year to year if you wish.

21.3. Renting Out in Joint Ownership

The exemption limit of £7,500 is reduced to £3,750 if during the tax year to April 5, someone else received income from letting accommodation in the same property.

This is likely to occur if you own a property in a partnership.

22. Generous Tax Breaks for Holiday Lets

In this section you will become familiar with the tax benefits associated with those who provide holiday lets.

There have been considerable changes to the Furnished Holiday Lettings (FHL) rules recently. First we start with the old rules:

22.1. Qualifying Criteria for a Holiday Let

If you let a property in a popular holiday location, e.g., the south coast, then you could well be operating a holiday lettings business. This is especially the case if your target market is people visiting and staying in your property for short periods of time.

In order to qualify your property as a holiday let, it must be fully furnished; that is, anyone moving into the property must be able to live out of the property without having to buy any additional furniture/furnishings.

It must also satisfy the following three conditions:

- the property must be available to let to the public on a commercial basis for at least 140 days;

- the property must be let for at least 70 days;

- let for periods of longer-term occupation (more than 31 consecutive days) for not more than 155 days during the year.

Income tax on a holiday let is charged in the same way as if you are operating a normal lettings business, where tax will be liable on any rental profits less expenses.

Holiday Lets

John buys a three-bedroom property in Bournemouth. His investment strategy is to rent the property in the summer periods to visiting holiday makers.

He offers the property for £250 per week.

Over the financial year, it is let for 35 weeks, which means that he has received a total rental income of £8,750. His expenses are £2,750.

This means that he is liable to pay tax on the £6,000 profit.

22.2. Three Generous Tax Benefits Associated With Holiday Lets

Operating a holiday letting business has three *significant* tax benefits. These are detailed below.

22.2.1. Offsetting losses against other income

If you are unfortunate enough to make a loss in your holiday lettings business, then the loss is treated as a trading loss and can be offset against any other source of income that you have, in the same way as trading losses.

Holiday Lets – Offsetting Losses

Kiran buys a property for the purpose of holiday letting for £130,000 in 1995.

Her first year of letting is very tough and she makes a £2,500 rental loss.

However because she is employed with a salary of £35,000, she is able to offset the loss against this income.

In other words she pays less tax on her employment income.

22.2.2. Re-investment of capital gains

If you decide to sell your holiday let and make a capital gain, then the sale proceeds can be re-invested into another qualifying asset, thus avoiding any immediate capital gains tax liability. This therefore means that you will not liable to pay any capital gains tax until you dispose of the asset you have re-invested in.

However, you can continue selling and re-investing the sale proceeds. By doing this, you will continue to defer any tax liability until the point at which you stop re-investing the sales proceeds.

Holiday Lets – Re-investment of Capital Gains

Continuing from the previous example.

Kiran sells her property 5 years later for £230,000, thus meaning she has made a profit of £100,000.

She buys another 'holiday let' property in the same tax year by re-investing the sale proceeds and therefore is able to defer any CGT liability.

22.2.3. FHL – new rules

- From 2009 FHL in the European Economic Area (EEA) qualified for the special rules available to FHL's in the UK, and from 2011 this became statutory.
- From 2012-3 the accommodation must be available to the public as holiday accommodation for at least 210 days, and actually let as such for at least 105 of those days.

- From April 2011 income from a FHL business (either in the UK or EEA) has to be computed separately from other property business income (again either in the UK or EEA) for the purposes of capital allowances, loss relief and relevant earnings for pension contributions.

- Trade loss reliefs used to be available, but from April 2011 loss relief is not available against general income. Losses can, therefore, only be set against income from the same UK or EEA FHL business.

23. Tax Implications When Converting Properties into Flats

This strategy has been written by Sarah Bradford.

Many a property developer has spotted the potential of buying a large property and converting it into flats in order to maximise profit. However, converting a property into flats for financial gain is not the sole preserve of the property developer.

A landlord may decide to convert a property into flats to maximise both rental income in the short term and profit on sale in the longer term. Likewise, a person may decide to convert a former family home into flats to realise the maximum possible gain on disposal. However, as is often the case, the tax implications will vary depending on the circumstances.

23.1. Scenario 1

A developer buys up a large house in a poor state of repair for £400,000. He spends a further £200,000 converting into four flats. The work takes six months. Once complete, the flats are sold for £250,000 each.

The nature of a property developer's trade is to develop properties for profit. As in this scenario the motive is to make a profit rather than to buy the property as an investment, any profit on sale is charged to income tax as a trading profit rather than to capital gains tax. The trading profit would be computed according to normal rules and the profit on this development (£400,000) would be taken into account in computing the developer's trading profits for the period in question.

As the developer is trading, capital gains tax (CGT) is not in point. Consequently, there is no CGT to pay when the flats are sold.

23.2. Scenario 2

A landlord has a number of properties that he lets out. He has owned a large property for a number of years which has been let out as a single dwelling. He decides to convert the property into flats. He then lets the flats for a further couple of years before selling them.

The landlord will be subject to CGT on any gain made from the sale of the flats. As the flats have always been let and have never been the landlord's main residence, neither private residence relief or letting relief are in point.

For the purposes of illustration, it is assumed that the landlord originally bought the house in 2005 for £300,000 and let it as a single unit until June 2009, when he converted the property into three flats. The conversion costs were £150,000. Each flat has two bedrooms and is approximately the same size.

The work was completed in November 2009 and the flats were again let until January 2011, when they were put on the market. Flat 1 sold in February 2011 for £220,000, Flat 2 also sold in February 2011 but for £230,000, and Flat 3 sold in March 2011 for £215,000. It is assumed that in each case the costs of sale are £2,000.

The gains on disposal are as follows:

Flat 1

Proceeds		£220,000
Less: cost of original property (1/3 x £300,000)	£100,000	
Conversion costs (1/3 x £150,000)	£50,000	
		(£150,000)
		£70,000
Less: costs of disposal		(£2,000)
Gain on sale		£68,000

Flat 2

Proceeds		£230,000
Less: cost of original property (1/3 x £300,000)	£100,000	
Conversion costs (1/3 x £150,000)	£50,000	
		(£150,000)
		£80,000
Less: costs of disposal		(£2,000)
Gain on sale		£78,000

Flat 3

Proceeds		£215,000
Less: cost of original property (1/3 x £300,000)	£100,000	
Conversion costs (1/3 x £150,000)	£50,000	
		(£150,000)
		£65,000
Less: costs of disposal		(£2,000)
Gain on sale		£63,000

The total gains on the sale of the flats (£209,000) will be taken into account in computing the landlord's net chargeable gains for 2010/11 and charged to CGT at the appropriate rate.

23.3. Scenario 3

After his children have grown up, a homeowner decides to convert his property into flats prior to sale to maximise the profit on sale. The flats are sold as soon as the work is complete.

For the purposes of illustration, it is assumed that the property was purchased in 1990 for £100,000. It was lived in as the taxpayer's main residence until June 2010, at which time work began to convert the property into three flats. The work was completed in

November 2010, and the flats were sold in January 2011 for £275,000 each. The conversion work cost £180,000.

At first sight, it may seem that the entire gain is covered by private residence relief as it had been the taxpayer's home throughout the period of ownership. However, there is a trap that will catch the unwary. This is because private residence relief is denied in respect of a gain in so far that it is attributable to any expenditure that is incurred after the beginning of a period of ownership that is incurred wholly or partly for the purposes of realising a gain.

Broadly, the provisions work to deny private residence relief in relation to that portion of the gain that is attributable to the expenditure incurred in order to realise a higher profit. It is therefore necessary to obtain a valuation of the house assuming the work had not been carried out and it was sold as a single dwelling. In this way, it is possible to establish the additional profit attributable to the conversion work.

In the above example, it is assumed that had the property been sold as the original family home it would have fetched £600,000. By converting it into flats, the sale proceeds increased to £825,000 (3 x £275,000). The cost attributable to the additional proceeds of £225,000 (i.e. £825,000 - £600,000) was the conversion expenditure of £180,000. This expenditure effectively generated an additional gain of £45,000 (£225,000 - £180,000). The development gain does not qualify for private residence relief.

The computation of the gain is therefore as follows:

	Total Gain £	Exempt Gain £	Non-Exempt Gain £
Proceeds	825,000	600,000	225,000
Less: cost of property	(100,000)	(100,000)	
cost of extension	(180,000)		(180,000)
GAIN	545,000	500,000	45,000

The non-exempt gain is reduced by the taxpayer's annual allowance to the extent that this remains available and charged to CGT at the appropriate rate.

23.4. Scenario 4

A homeowner decides that her house is too big for her. She converts it into two flats, one of which she sells. She continues to live in the remaining flat.

The property was purchased in 2000 for £325,000. In 2010, the property was converted into two flats. The conversion work was completed in May 2010. One flat was sold in June 2010 for £275,000. The conversion costs were £40,000. At that date, the value of the unconverted house was £500,000 and the value of the flat retained was £350,000.

The combined value of the two flats at the date the flat was sold was £625,000. This is £125,000 more than the value of the unconverted property at that date. The conversion costs are £40,000, giving rise to a gain attributable to conversion of £85,000.

This gain is not covered by the private residence exemption. However, it must be attributed between the flats to ascertain the amount that comes into charge in respect of the sale of the first flat. This is done simply on an apportionment basis by reference to the relative values of each property on the date that the first flat was sold.

The non-exempt gain attributable to the flat sold is therefore:

£275,000/£625,000 x £85,000 = £37,400.

The remainder of the gain attributable to the first flat is covered by private residence relief.

The non-exempt gain (as reduced by any allowable losses and the annual exemption to the extent that it remains available) is charged to CGT at the appropriate rate (18% or 28% depending on whether the taxpayer is a higher rate taxpayer).

The balance of the non-exempt gain will come into charge on the eventual sale of the flat which has become the taxpayer's home.

How to Slash Your Property Capital Gains Tax

24. Understanding Capital Gains Tax (CGT)

Before we look at the different ways to cut your capital gains tax saving strategies, it is important to understand what is meant by the term **capital gains tax (CGT)** and when property investors are liable to pay it.

In this section you will become familiar with CGT and how it is calculated when you decide to sell your property.

24.1. When You Are Liable to Pay CGT

A property investor is likely to incur a CGT liability in the following two situations:

a) when a property is sold at a higher price than for which it was purchased;

b) when a property, or part of a property, is transferred to a non-spouse.

> Properties and other assets can be transferred between husband and wife freely, without triggering a CGT liability.

Both of the above situations are illustrated in the following case studies.

CGT Liability When Selling a Property

Maria purchases a buy-to-let property in January 1998 for £100,000. She rents it out for five years and then sells it for £210,000.

This means that she has made a capital gain of £110,000, upon which she is liable to pay CGT.

CGT Liability When Transferring a Property

Maria purchases a buy-to-let property in January 1998 for £100,000. She rents it out for five years and then gifts the property to her mother.

She receives no payment from her mother for the property.

Although Maria has received no payment for the property, she is treated as having transferred the property to her mother at 'market value,' which is £210,000. Therefore, again, Maria is liable to pay CGT on the £110,000 profit.

> Property dealers/traders are not liable to pay CGT. When they sell a property, the profit is classed as a dealing profit, and therefore they are liable to pay **income tax** on the profits.

24.2. Why Delaying Exchanging Contracts Can Defer Your Tax Bill

There is a common misconception that the tax date for a sale of a property is the completion date of a property. This is not true. The tax date for CGT purposes is actually the date the contracts are exchanged.

Exchange of Contracts

Terry decides to sell his property and advertises it for £220,000 in January 2012. An offer is accepted in the first week of February.

Terry knows that if he exchanges contracts before the 6th April 2012, then any tax that is due will need to be paid by 31st January 2013.

However if he delays the exchange of contracts till the 6th April, then the sale will be considered to have fallen in the 2012-2013 tax year and therefore no tax will be due until 31st January 2014.

He draws out the sales proceedings so that the exchange of contracts is done on the 6th April and the completion a couple of days after.

24.3. Recent History and Changes to the CGT Rate

October 2007
In the October 2007 pre-budget report, Chancellor Alistair Darling announced that a flat rate CGT rate of 18% would be introduced from April 6th 2008.

March 2008
The announcement in the October 2007 pre-budget report was confirmed in the March 2008 budget and became effective from 6th April 2008.

What this meant was that any property sold from 6th April 2008 would only pay a flat rate capital gains tax of 18%, regardless of the size of profit.

It was no surprise that a number of commentators referred to the March 2008 budget as a budget for the **property investor!**

June 22nd 2010
In the 22 June 2010 Budget Chancellor George Osborne announced new CGT rates. Capital gains made on disposals from 23 June 2010 onwards are added to the taxpayers other income.

Any gains falling below the higher rate threshold are taxed at 18%. Any gains falling above the threshold are taxed at 28%.

Trusts pay capital gains tax at only one rate – 28%.

In the March 2016 budget the Chancellor reduced the rates of capital gains tax to 20% for a higher rate taxpayer, and 10% for a basic rate taxpayer. However, a capital gain on the sale of a residential property will still be subject to the old rates of 28% and 18%.

24.4. How Your CGT Bill is Calculated

Calculating the tax liability on the sale or transfer of a property is not easy.

Given the property price increases over the past few years alone, investors are sitting on significant capital gains.

It is important to realise that a number of reliefs and strategies are available to reduce any CGT liability you may have. The most significant of these are detailed in the remainder of this guide.

However, listed in the table below are the typical reliefs/reductions that can be claimed when a property is sold/transferred.

If applicable, these can be offset against the capital gain made on the property and can be used to significantly reduce any tax liability.

Relief/Reduction	Description
Buying and Selling Costs	Typical purchase costs include • solicitor' fees; • mortgage booking fee; • survey costs; • cost of searches, e.g., land, mining, etc. Typical selling costs include • agency fees; • solicitor' fees; • redemption penalties, etc. See section 29.3 for further details.
Capital Costs	If you have made costs of a capital nature, then these can also be offset. A capital cost is one that has increased the price of the property.

	Examples of capital costs include the building of conservatories, additional bedrooms, loft conversions, garage conversions, etc.
Indexation Relief	This relief was available for qualifying for property that was sold before April 6th 2008.
Private Residence Relief	This relief is based on the period that the property was classed as your PPR. See sections 25, 27 & 28 for further details.
Private Letting Relief	This relief is a very generous relief that can reduce your capital gain by up to an additional £40,000. See section 26.3 for further details.
Allowable Losses	If you have incurred capital losses, then these can be offset against any capital gain made when you dispose of your property. See section 29.2 for further details.
Taper Relief	This relief was introduced in April 1998 and was a replacement for indexation relief. However it can only be claimed for property sold before 6th April 2008.
Personal CGT Allowance	For the tax years 2015-16 and 2016-17 the personal CGT allowance is £11,100. See section 29.1 for further details.

25. Private Residence Relief'

In this section you will become familiar with the extremely powerful **private residence relief**.

This allowance on its own can wipe out tens or even hundreds of thousands of pounds off your chargeable capital gains.

25.1. What is Private Residence Relief?

This relief is available to you if you have lived in a property that has been classed as your **main residence** for a period of time.

This relief is not available to you if you are a property dealer and purchased a property with the sole intention of making a dealing profit, i.e., you did not make it your main residence.

The technical name for a person's main residence is **principle private residence (PPR)**.

> If you have lived in a property that has been your PPR, then you are not liable to pay any capital gains tax on the price appreciation that is attributed to the period when you lived in the property.

There are two types of residence relief that are available, and both are described and illustrated in the following two sections.

25.1.1. Full residence relief

If the property has been classed as your PPR throughout your period of ownership, then you can claim **full residence relief**.

If you can claim full residence relief, then this means that you will have no CGT liability. This is regardless of the capital profit you have made on the property.

Every homeowner who has occupied their property since the first day of ownership up until the time of sale is entitled to use this relief.

Full Residence Relief

Alex buys his first home in May 1990 for £65,000. He lives in it from the day of purchase up until the day he sells it in June 2001. The selling price is £150,000, which means that he has made a capital profit of £85,000. He is not liable to pay any tax on this profit as he is able to claim full residence relief because the property was his main residence during his period of ownership.

25.1.2. Partial residence relief

You are able to claim **partial residence relief** if your property has been your main residence for a period of time but not for the whole period of ownership.

If you are claiming partial residence relief, then the amount of relief you can claim is determined by dividing the periods when the property was classed as your PPR by the total periods of ownership.

For example, if you purchased a property, let it out for 7 years and then lived in it for three years before selling it then you will be able to claim 3/10 partial residence relief. This is because you owned the property for 10 years, but it was your main residence for three of those years.

You are most likely to claim partial residence relief if

- you have a second home (see section 28 for more details on how you can legitimately reduce your tax liability by nominating your main residence);

- you are a property investor who has let a property after having previously lived in it.

25.2. How Long in a Property Before It Can Be Classed as My PPR?

This is one of the most commonly asked tax questions.

The reason for the popularity of this question is because if you can prove that a property was genuinely your PPR, you can make use of some very generous tax reliefs. You will see in the following strategies exactly how you can use these reliefs to your advantage to reduce or even wipe out any tax liability.

HMRC have not given any specific guidance as to how long you need to live in a property before you can claim that it has been your principle private residence.

However, as a general rule of thumb, you should try to make it your permanent residence for at least one year, i.e., 12 months.

The longer you live in a property, the better chance you have of claiming residence relief.

HMRC are not necessarily interested in how long you lived in the property. They are *much more* interested in whether the property really was your home and whether you *really* did live in the property!

If you want to claim this relief, here are some pointers that will help you to convince the taxman that a property genuinely was your private residence.

a) Have utility and other bills in your own name at the property address.

Typical bills will include
i. gas bills;
ii. water rates;

iii. electricity supply bills;
iv. council tax bills;
v. TV licence, etc.

b) Make the property address your voting address on the electoral register.

c) Be able to demonstrate that you bought furniture and furnishings for the property. Keep receipts and prove that bulky furniture was delivered to the property address.

d) Have all bank statements delivered to the property address.

By following the above guidelines, you will be in a good position to convince the taxman that a property was genuinely your home.

25.3. More Insight into What Makes A PPR

This strategy has been written by James Bailey.

A case heard by the Tax Tribunal (AJ Clarke v HMRC) has shed more light on what it takes to make a property your 'main residence' and thus exempt from capital gains tax (CGT).

Mr Clarke lived with his wife and children at Oaks Farm. His marriage was failing and he wanted to get his children away from his wife's influence. He bought 60 Nayland Road in July 2002 and moved in with his children. He had used a short term loan to buy it and needed to raise money to pay off the loan, so he obtained planning permission to build another property (58a) in the garden of No 60.

He put No 60 on the market in December 2002, only 5 months after buying it, and it sold in March 2003. He moved in with his mother while 58a was completed, and was able to occupy it in July 2003.

In July 2005, he had to move back to Oaks Farm, as his (now divorced) wife had attempted suicide and he felt he had to be there. Number 58a was put on the market and sold in November 2005.

HMRC argued that neither of the Nayland Road properties had ever been his main residence and were thus not exempt from CGT. They pointed out that he had not notified anyone of his changes of address, and correspondence for him continued to be sent to him at Oaks Farm, where he had an office from which he ran his business.

They also argued that the use of the short term loan to buy No 60 indicated that he bought it with the intention of selling it and developing another property in the garden – which of course is what he had in fact done.

Although HMRC grudgingly accepted that Mr Clarke had in fact resided at both of the Nayland Road properties, they said that his residence in both of them was merely a temporary measure and not intended to be the start of a new 'permanent home' – an expression that does not appear in the legislation, but one HMRC are fond of using in these disputes.

Mr Clarke could have made life much easier for himself if he had written to HMRC within two years of moving into No 60, nominating it as his main residence, and then done the same again when he moved into No 58a, but he had not done so within the two year time limit, so the question of which property was his main residence had to be decided on the facts.

Normally, a married couple can only have one main residence between them. The case report does not make it clear, but I assume that HMRC accepted that they were permanently separated at the time Mr Clarke bought No 60, so that potentially Mr Clarke could have a main residence of his own.

If Mr Clarke had come to me for advice, I would probably have said he had a good case as far as No 58a was concerned, as he had lived there for a couple of years, but that HMRC would probably win the argument on No 60, given how he had financed the purchase and how quickly he had put it on the market.

In fact, the Tribunal accepted that both 60 and 58a had been Mr Clarke's main residence while he occupied them, and so the gains on the sales were exempt from CGT.

They based their decision on the fact that they accepted Mr Clarke's evidence of what he had intended at the time he bought No 60 (to live there and to sell part of the land to repay the loan – the idea of building 58a had been suggested to him later by his business partner).

Practical Tip
The above case makes it clear that your intention when buying and moving into a property is the crucial factor in deciding whether it becomes your main residence, even if events subsequently lead you to change your mind.

25.4. Private Residence CGT Exemption - How To Lose It!

James Bailey highlights a potential problem with some claims for capital gains tax main residence relief.

The capital gains tax (CGT) legislation which provides for relief on the disposal of a private residence includes a provision (in TCGA 1992, s 224(3)) which appears to deny the normal exemption for capital gains on a 'main residence' if you hoped to sell it at a profit when you bought it.

At the first reading, section 224 (3) seems to do away with almost all the CGT exemption. It says the main residence exemption:

"...shall not apply in relation to a gain if the acquisition of, or of the interest in, the dwelling-house or the part of a dwelling-house was made wholly or partly for the purpose of realising a gain from the disposal of it, and shall not apply in relation to a gain so far as attributable to any expenditure which was incurred after the beginning of the period of ownership and was incurred wholly or partly for the purpose of realising a gain from the disposal" (emphasis added).

Notice those two uses of 'or partly'- most of us hope to sell our homes at a profit one day, and adverts for home improvements like conservatories often make the point that this will increase the value of the property concerned. So are we all doomed to pay tax when we sell our homes? Fortunately, HMRC's Capital Gains manual instructs its staff to behave reasonably and not use the legislation in cases like these:

"It would be unreasonable and restrictive to apply the legislation in this way. The subsection should only be taken to apply when the primary purpose of the acquisition, or of the expenditure, was an early disposal at a profit" (CG65210).

HMRC generally use the legislation in three situations:

1. Quasi property development
It is difficult for HMRC to establish that someone who buys a run-down house, does it up, and then sells it in a short period of time is trading as a property developer if he genuinely lives in the property while he does so, and he has no other residence at the time, but they may use section 224(3) to charge CGT on the profit made.

2. Leasehold Enfranchisement
Tenants under a lease may get the opportunity to buy the freehold from their landlord. This is generally a sensible investment, but if you then sell the freehold shortly afterwards, you may find section 224(3) rears its head, as far as the gain attributable to the freehold is concerned.

3. Extensions and conversions
A house divided into flats will often sell for more than the same house undivided. If you do this (or build an extension) shortly before sale, then some of the gain may not be exempt.

4. Calculating the lost exemption
Except in the case of the 'property developer', it is not all of the gain that is taxed; it is only the part relating to the offending expenditure. This involves a valuation exercise.

For example, imagine a house converted into three flats and immediately sold. Each flat sells for £150,000, whereas the unconverted house would have sold for £350,000. The conversion work cost £50,000. The taxable gain is as follows:

Sale proceeds of three flats at £150,000 each	£450,000
Estimate of sale proceeds of unconverted house	(£350,000)
Gain attributable to conversion	£100,000
Less cost of conversion	(£50,000)
Taxable gain	£50,000

The longer the period between the expenditure and the sale, the less risk there is of section 224(3) being trotted out, especially if you can show another reason for the expenditure (an extension for a growing family, for example).

Practical Tip
Do not let section 224(3) put you off sensible expenditure to enhance the value of your home. In the example above, assuming the £11,000 annual CGT exempt amount is available, the CGT payable is, at worst, under £11,100 (less if the property is jointly owned), so you are still better off for doing the conversion.

26. The EASIEST Way to Legitimately Avoid CGT

In this section you will learn about two key CGT saving reliefs that are available to property investors.

These two reliefs are known as the
- 18-month rule (previously known as the '36-month rule') and
- private letting relief.

26.1. The old '36-Month Rule'

Up until 5th April 2014, if a house has at some time been your **main residence**, the last three years of ownership are always treated as though you lived there (for the purposes of working out the number of PPR years in the capital gains tax calculation).

This is the case even if you didn't actually live there in those last three years.

26.2. The new '18-Month Rule'

From 6th April 2014, the rule has now become the '18-month rule'. This means that if a property has at some time been your **main residence**, then the last 18 months are now only treated as though you lived there.

The case study below shows how this rule can be used to provide residence relief.

Using the 18-Month Rule to Get Full Residence Relief

Joanne buys an apartment in London docklands in 1990 for £100,000.

She lives in the apartment for ten years before she decides to move in with her long-term boyfriend. She rents her apartment for 12 months and then sells it 6 months later.

The apartment is sold in 2002 for £250,000.

Joanne will have no CGT liability on the profit of £150,000 as she is able to claim full residence relief; that is, her entire 11 and a half years of ownership is exempt from CGT. This is because for 10 years the property was her PPR and therefore there is no CGT liability on this period of ownership.

Also, she is able to claim the **18-month rule**, which means that the last 18 months of ownership i.e. when the property was let are also exempt from CGT.

26.3. Wiping Out CGT by Using Private Letting Relief

> If you still have a taxable capital gain after using the 18-month rule, then it is possible that any tax liability can be eliminated by using the **private letting relief**.

HMRC state that the private letting relief can be used where

- you sell a dwelling house which is, or has been, your only or main residence, and

- part or all of it has at some time in your period of ownership been let as a residential accommodation.

The amount of private letting relief that can be claimed cannot be greater than £40,000, and it must be the lowest of the following three values:

- £40,000;

- the amount of private residence relief that has already been claimed;

- the amount of any chargeable gain that is made due to the letting; that is, this is the amount that is attributed to the increase in the property value during the period it was let.

The use of this relief is best illustrated via the following case study.

Private Letting Relief

Roger buys a three-bedroom semi-detached house in North Wales for £50,000 in 1990.

He lives in the house for two years and then decides to move to a bigger four-bedroom detached house. He rents out the three-bedroom house for the next five years.

In 1997 he sells the three-bedroom house for £120,000. This means that he has made a capital gain of £70,000.

5/7ths of the profit is exempt from CGT because he is able to claim partial residence relief (two years PPR and the 36-month rule).

This means that he is only liable to pay CGT on the remaining £20,000 of chargeable gain. However, Roger is also able to claim private letting relief, and the amount he can claim is the lowest of the following three values:

- £40,000;
- amount of private residence relief already claimed is £50,000;

- amount of any chargeable gain that is made due to the letting is £20,000 (assuming that property increased by £10,000 in each of the two years that the property was let).

This means that Roger is allowed to claim private letting relief of £20,000 as this is the lowest of the three values.

Therefore the outstanding chargeable gain of £20,000 is cancelled out by this relief, which means that he has absolutely no CGT liability.

In other words, Roger has made a tax-free capital gain of £70,000 just by having lived in a property for two years!

In this section you have come across two of the most powerful CGT reduction strategies available to property investors—make sure you consider them both before you decide to sell your property!

27. Increasing Property Value and Avoiding Tax

In this section you will become familiar with a tax relief that allows you to claim capital gains relief on the first 12 months of property ownership.

You will also learn how property developers are taking advantage of this relief to grow property portfolios without incurring a CGT liability.

27.1. No CGT on the First 12 Months of Ownership

More and more investors are increasingly facing a situation where they purchase a property but are unable to occupy it immediately due to a variety of legitimate reasons.

- You are having the property built, or

- You are altering or re-decorating the property, or

- You remain in your old home whilst you are selling it.

If you are unable to move into the property immediately after you have purchased it, then it is possible to claim 12 months relief. What this means is that the first 12 months of ownership will still be exempt from any capital gains tax. This is regardless of whether you currently have another property that is your main residence.

However, in order to claim this relief, you *must* occupy the property within 12 months of the purchase. And a condition of the relief is that after moving in you stay in the property long enough for it to become your qualifying main residence.

First 12 Months of Ownership

Asif lives with his family in a two-bedroom terraced house.

In January 1998 he buys a run-down three-bedroom semi-detached property that requires a significant amount of development and modernisation. The property is purchased for £70,000.

The development and modernisation work starts in February 1998 and is completed 10 months later, in December 1998. The total cost of the project is £20,000.

Before he moves into the property with his family, Asif has the property valued at £120,000. This means that the property has appreciated by £30,000 (i.e., 120,000 − (£70,000 + £20,000)).

There will be no tax liability on the gain of £30,000. This is because for the purposes of working out the number of PPR years in the capital gains tax calculation the first year can be treated as though Asif and his family actually lived in the property.

27.2. Using the Rule to Grow a Portfolio without Paying CGT

Using the **first 12 months of ownership rule** is quite an effective property tax–saving strategy for builders and property developers. This is because they are able to build/develop a property whilst living out of another property. When the new property is ready, they are able to rent out or sell the existing property before moving into the new property.

Exploiting the First 12 Months of Ownership Rule

Alex is a property builder by trade who lives out of his two-bedroom apartment.

He decides to build his own three-bedroom detached house. The house is completed within 12 months of purchasing the land, so he decides to rent out the apartment and move into the new three-bedroom house.

Three years later, he sells the apartment and buys another piece of land, and this time he builds a four-bedroom property. Again, it is built and occupied within 12 months, and again he rents out the existing property.

Alex carries on with this cycle of selling his let property and buying land every four years in order to build a bigger house, which he occupies within 12 months.

On the sale of each property Alex will have no CGT liability. This is because

- the first 12 months will be exempt from tax;
- the time he lives in the property will also be exempt from CGT;
- and the last three years of ownership will also be exempt from CGT.

The tax strategy demonstrated in the above case study illustrates how you can quite effectively grow a portfolio and avoid having a CGT liability. However, as demonstrated in the case study, you would need to be prepared to relocate every four to five years to take advantage of the tax-free gain.

This strategy can be used equally well for property developers who buy run-down properties and then move into them before moving onto the next project.

Be wary of HMRC!
By using the above strategy, Alex will be able to avoid paying CGT as he is genuinely living in a property for a decent period of time, i.e., 4 years. If you try to adopt such a strategy on a smaller timescale, i.e., where you move more frequently, then HMRC may well challenge your motive, and you may be liable to pay income tax on the sale of your properties—**so be warned**!

28. Nominating Residence to Avoid CGT

In this section you will understand how people with more than one family home can limit or even avoid CGT on the sale of their second homes.

28.1. Having More Than One Family Home

If you have purchased a second home over the past years, it is extremely likely that you will face a considerable CGT liability when you decide to sell it.

A common scenario for having a second home is if you live in a city/town that is close to your place of work but also own a property where you go to spend your vacations, e.g., on the southeast coast of England.

If you are able to own multiple homes, then you may well save a considerable amount of tax by nominating your residence to HMRC.

28.2. Nominating Your Residence to HMRC

If you decide to sell a property, consider nominating it as your main residence to save on tax.

In order to make a nomination you must:

a) inform HMRC in writing which property is your main residence;
b) make the nomination within two years after acquiring the second property.

> **REMEMBER:** A property cannot be nominated as your main residence if it is let out.

The following case study demonstrates how a potential CGT liability can be wiped out by nominating a different residence.

Switching Residence to Avoid CGT

Bill lives in a two-bedroom apartment in London and works as a stock broker in the heart of the city centre. He purchased his apartment in June 1995.

In June 1999 he also decides to buy a semi-detached three-bedroom house in Southampton that is just by the coast. He starts to spend most of his weekends there with his girlfriend.

In April 2001 Bill realises that his house in Southampton has significantly increased in value and that he will face a considerable CGT liability if he decides to sell.

He takes professional advice and is told to nominate his house in Southampton as his main residence.

He therefore notifies HMRC in writing that the house in Southampton is his 'nominated' main residence. This is done in June 2001 and means that the house is treated as his main residence from June 1999[4].

Bill decides to sell the house in June 2003 for a £150,000 profit and has no CGT liability. This is because

a) the house is exempt for the first two years because it has been nominated as his main residence;
b) the last two years are exempt due to the old 36-month rule

Once the house has been sold, Bill notifies HMRC that his London apartment is now his main residence from June 2001 (i.e., from two years ago). This means that when he sells his apartment in June 2005, 8/10ths of partial residence relief can be claimed.

This is determined as follows.

- Bill has owned the apartment for 10 years.

- Four years partial residence relief is due because between June 1995 and June 1999 it was his classed as his main residence.

- An additional four years partial residence relief is due because between June 2001 and June 2005 it was again classed as his main residence.

This means that by switching and nominating his main residence, Bill has totally avoided any CGT liability on his three-bedroom house and also achieved a considerable reduction in the capital gain on his London apartment.

---

[4]A principle private residence election can be backdated to take effect at a date two years before the date of the election

29. Other Ways to Reduce Your CGT Bill

In this section you will learn how you can reduce your CGT liability even further by

- using your annual CGT allowance;
- offsetting previous capital losses;
- timing the sale of your property.

29.1. Using Your Annual CGT Allowance

Each individual has a capital gains tax allowance that can be claimed in the tax year. What this means is that if you have made a capital gain on the sale of an asset, then you can offset the CGT allowance for the tax year in which the asset was sold.

When making a sale with a capital gain, it is important to understand the following two key points:

- if the entire allowance has already been claimed in the tax year, then it cannot be claimed again in the same tax year;

- if part of the allowance has already been claimed in the tax year, then only the outstanding unclaimed amount can be claimed.

The CGT allowances for the current and previous tax years are detailed in the table below.

	Tax Year	
	2015-2016	**2016-2017**
CGT Allowance	£11,100	£11,100

The following case study helps to explain how the allowance can be used:

Claiming the Entire Personal CGT Allowance

Bill sells his investment property on 10th April 2015 and has a £12,100 capital gain.

The only tax allowance he is able to claim is his personal CGT allowance, which is £11,100 for 2015–2016, and to date, this has not been claimed.

This means that after this allowance has been deducted from his capital gain (i.e., £12,100 – £11,100) he is liable to pay tax on the remaining gain of £1,000.

If Bill sells another qualifying asset with a capital gain in the 2015–2016 tax year, then he is not able to use his personal CGT allowance again.

This is because the entire CGT allowance for that tax year has already been used.

Claiming Partial Personal CGT Allowance

Samantha sells her investment property on 10th April 2015 and has a £6,000 capital gain.

The only tax allowance she is able to claim is his personal CGT allowance, which is £11,100 for 2015–2016, and to date, this has not been claimed.

This means that she has no a CGT liability as the allowance of £11,100 is greater than her £6,000 gain. Furthermore, she still has £5,100 remaining from the allowance that can be used if she decides to sell another property or qualifying asset

29.2. Capital Losses

If you have made losses on previous 'qualifying' assets, then you can register these losses with HMRC and offset these against any future capital gains.

Examples of 'qualifying' assets include

- property (e.g., you have a number of residential investment properties);
- shares in a company (e.g., you have shares in Lloyds Bank);
- units in a unit trust.

> If you have made any losses, inform HMRC of the losses in the tax year in which they were incurred. For example, if you made a loss in a share-trading deal in May 2009, then register this with HMRC in the 2009–2010 tax return.

If you are unable to or you forget to register your losses, you can still claim these losses up to four years after the end of the tax year in which the loss occurred.

This is illustrated in the following case study.

Claiming Partial Personal CGT Allowance

Louise buys £20,000 of shares in Marconi at the height of the technology boom in May 2000. Unfortunately, the share price crumbles, and she ends up selling the shares 12 months later for a total value of £200.

This means that she has made a loss of £19,800.

She is unaware that she can register this loss with HMRC so that it can be offset against any future capital gain.

Had she known, she would have registered this loss in her 2001–2002 tax return.

After her misfortunes in the stock market, Louise decides to focus on property instead and buys an apartment in Birmingham in June 2001 for £120,000. She decides to sell it in June 2004 for £170,000. This gives her a capital gain of £50,000.

She takes tax advice and is told by her advisor that she is still able to register her losses with HMRC. In fact, as long as she registers the losses with HMRC by 5 April 2005, they can be offset against any future capital gain.

This means that she can reduce her taxable gain on the sale of the property by £19,800 immediately.

If you have made any losses on qualifying assets, then make sure that they are registered with HMRC!

29.3. Buying and Selling Costs

What many property investors fail to realise is that if you have incurred costs when buying and selling your property, then these can also be offset when the property is sold.

Typical buying costs will include

- solicitors fees;
- surveyor costs;
- land registry fees;
- solicitor's indemnity insurance;
- local authority searches, etc.

Typical selling costs will include

- solicitors fees;
- estate agency fees;
- advertising costs;
- accountancy fees, etc.

29.4. Selling at the Right Time Can Save You Tax!

The time when you decide to sell a property can have a significant bearing on how much tax you will save.

Before you sell your property, make sure you consider the following key pointer.

a) Beginning/end of tax year

If you expect to dispose of a number of capital assets in the same year, then try to sell them in different years to make use of your annual CGT allowance.

With just some simple tax planning you can phase the selling of assets to make sure that you always utilise your CGT allowance.

In particular, try to make sure you use up your annual CGT allowance before the end of the tax year. This is especially the case if you intend to sell multiple assets.

Timing the Sale of Your Property

John owns two buy-to-let properties, and in January 2014 he decides to sell them both so he can reinvest the money into a different area. John believes that he can achieve better returns by investing into an area of major regeneration.

He puts both properties on the market, and a sale is agreed on both of them.

John agrees with the vendors that the sale of one property will be completed in the 2013–2014 tax year so that he can use the CGT allowance of £10,900 for that year.

He also agrees that for the second property, the contracts will be exchanged in the second week of April 2014, again so that he can use the CGT allowance of £11,000 for the 2014–2015 tax year.

If John had sold the properties in the same tax year, then he would only have been able to use the CGT allowance on the sale of one of the properties.

30. Using Property Partnerships to Cut Your CGT bill

In section 6 you saw how it was possible to set up property partnerships and how they could be effectively used to reduce your income tax liability.

In this section you will learn how property partnerships can also be used to minimise your capital gains tax liability.

30.1. Making Use of Multiple CGT Allowances

One of the biggest tax benefits of a property partnership is that each person in the partnership can use his/her annual personal CGT allowance when the property is sold.

Using Property Partnerships to Save CGT (1)

Mr and Mrs Jamieson purchased a three-bedroom detached house in March 1999 for £175,000.

They decide to sell the property in May 2015 for £300,000.

They have not used the annual CGT allowance for the year, so they are able to each claim their annual allowance of £11,100.

It does not matter how many partners there are as each partner will be allowed to use his/her personal CGT allowance, as long as it has not been used up on the sale of another qualifying asset.

30.2. Save Tax by Transferring to Your Husband/Wife or Civil Partner

In the previous section, it became evident that if you transfer/gift an asset, CGT may be due on any gain made at the time of transfer.

In this section you will become familiar with methods for transferring property between husband and wife to reduce tax.

DON'T FORGET: Property ownership can be transferred freely between husband and wife.

30.2.1. Transferring to lower-rate taxpayer

In the following sections, references to 'higher rate taxpayers' and 'lower rate taxpayers' are only relevant to disposals before 6 April 2008 and after 22 June 2010 when the rate of capital gains tax is dependent on the amount of other income the taxpayer received in the tax year of disposal. As detailed in section 24.3, between 5

April 2008 and 22 June 2010 all capital gains were taxed at a flat rate of 18%, independent of the taxpayers other income.

If your spouse is a lower-rate taxpayer, then consider moving a greater share of the property ownership into his/her name before the property is sold.

This is especially the case if you are a higher-rate taxpayer and your spouse has minimal income.

30.2.2. Transferring if partner has registered losses

In section 29.2 you learned that if you registered any capital losses, then you could offset any future capital gain on your property against these losses.

However, if your spouse has made losses in his/her sole name, then you can transfer part or the entire property into his/her name to offset the losses against the gain.

Transferring When a Spouse Has Registered Losses

Mr and Mrs Karim bought a three-bedroom detached house in 2001 for £150,000 on a buy-to-let basis. Both are higher-rate taxpayers.

Prior to the purchase, Mr Karim had actively and unsuccessfully traded on the stock market and had run up losses of £50,000. He had registered the losses with HMRC.

In May 2012 they decide to sell the property and invest in the northwest, where they feel they can achieve a better rental income and also higher capital growth.

They decide to sell the property, and it sells for £207,000, thus giving them a capital gain of £57,000.

Prior to the sale the property is moved into the sole name of Mr Karim. By doing this, they have both successfully avoided any CGT liability.

This is because:
   a) Mr Karim can offset the £50,000 of losses that he accumulated through his share dealings;
   b) the remaining amount of £7,000 is consumed by his personal CGT allowance for 2012-2013.

If Mr and Mrs Karim had continued to own the property as a 50:50 split, they would have had a higher tax liability. This is because Mrs Karim would have been liable to pay tax on £17,900 (after the personal CGT allowance for 2012-2013 of £10,600 has been deducted). (Mr Karim has his brought forward losses available to him, so he has no tax liability).

30.3. Transferring Strategies for Non-spouse and Non-civil Partnerships

In this section you will become familiar with important considerations you need to make before transferring to a non-spouse.

30.3.1. Transferring in stages

A good tax planning strategy for avoiding or minimising CGT is to transfer the property ownership in stages.

If you do this, then you can use your annual CGT allowance over a number of years to avoid CGT.

Transferring in Stages

Mr and Mrs Higginbottom purchased an investment property for £40,000 in 1998. They are both higher-rate taxpayers.

Their long-term intention is to give the property to their son to help him get onto the property ladder. At the time of purchase they appreciate that they may well have to pay CGT on the transfer at a later date if the property price has increased.

So, they decide to start transferring ownership by using up their annual CGT allowance. From 1999–2002 they transfer accumulated property capital gain on the property to their son using their combined annual CGT allowance.

By transferring the property in stages and using their annual CGT allowances, they have successfully avoided paying CGT on the property.

DON'T FORGET: Each individual is entitled to use the annual CGT allowance to legitimately reduce their CGT bill. Don't let the allowance go to waste, especially if you know to whom you will be transferring property ownership in the future.

30.4. Transferring at 'Arm's Length'

It is important to understand that whenever a property is transferred or sold to a 'connected person,' the estimated market value at the time of sale/transfer must be used when calculating the CGT liability, instead of the amount paid.

This is because transactions between such people are automatically treated as not being at arm's length.

Connected persons are defined as

- business partners;
- mother, father, or more remote ancestor;
- daughter, son, or more remote descendant;

- brothers and/or sisters;
- those who are regarded as close family by marriage, i.e., in-laws.

Sale Not at Arm's Length

Rebecca buys a property in 1980 for £75,000. Its market value in January 2003 is £350,000.

She decides to sell the property to her younger sister, Aleesha, at a significantly reduced price of £200,000.

It is clear that the transaction is between connected persons and therefore is treated as not having been made at arm's length.

Therefore Rebecca will be taxed as though she has received £350,000 from the sale of the property.

---

31. Advanced Strategies for Avoiding CGT

This strategy outlines a number of additional reliefs that are available, which can help to reduce the CGT liability further in certain scenarios.

Please Note: From April 2015 the rules applying when a non UK resident sells a UK residential property, and the rules for UK capital gains tax when he does so, have changed. See the chapter: **Essential Tax Advice for International Property Investors**.

31.1. How to Claim an Additional Three Years of PPR

If you live in a property and then vacate it but return to live in the property again, you can claim up to three years relief. This is known as the **three years' absence relief**.

It is not necessary for the property to have been rented out during the period that it was vacated.

However, for the three years absence relief (sandwiched between periods of actual residence) it does matter if another property was your PPR during those three years, i.e. both properties cannot be your PPR at the same time.

Claiming Additional Three Years' Absence Relief

John buys a two-bedroom property in Manchester in 1985 for £45,000 and lives in it for 10 years.

He then rents a two-bedroom house in London in 1995. He decides to rent out the house in Manchester.

He moves back to Manchester in 1998 (after three years). For the period 1995-1998, John informs HMRC that the Manchester house was his elected main residence, since he was renting in London

When John moves back to Manchester he lives there for an additional three years and then sells the property in 2001 for £250,000.

This means that the property ownership can be summarised as follows:

- 1985 to 1995 he lived in the property
- 1995 to 1998 he rented the property
- 1998 to 2001 he returned to live in the property again

This means that John has no CGT liability when he sells the property.

This is because for thirteen years the property was his main residence. Also, he is able to claim the three years absence relief when the property was rented out.

Therefore John has made a £205,000 tax-free capital profit!

31.2. Claiming PPR When Working Overseas

If you lived in a property and your employer required you to work overseas, then the period that you spent working overseas can also be claimed as residential relief. This relief can be claimed if you return to the same property and make it your **main residence again**. The time that you spent working overseas is irrelevant.

However, you can only claim this relief if no other residence qualifies for relief during the absence, i.e., you had no other nominated PPR.

Claiming PPR When Working Overseas

Alex buys a two-bedroom house in 1990 for £130,000.

He works as an IT consultant, and in 1992 he is asked to work on a three-year project in the United States. He jumps at the opportunity and decides to let his property whilst working overseas. His work permit is extended and he returns to live in the house in 1999, after seven years.

For the period 1992-1999, Alex informs HMRC that the two-bedroom house was his elected main residence.

In 2003 he is offered a permanent position in the United States, which he accepts, so he decides to sell his UK property. He has it valued at £300,000.

Alex will have no CGT liability because:

- between 1990 and 1992 he lived in the property, so there is no CGT liability;
- between 1992 and 1999 he could still claim residence relief as he was working outside the country;
- between 1999 and 2003 the property was again his main residence.

Even if Alex had bought a property in the United States in 1992, since he elected for the UK property to be his PPR, he could still claim relief on the UK property under both overseas employment relief and the last three years' ownership relief. If he had not elected to make the UK property his PPR, then he could not claim relief for the years 1992-1999.

31.3. Claiming PPR When Re-locating in the UK

If you live in a property and then your employer requires you to work elsewhere in the UK, then you can claim up to four years' relief. You must return to the property and make it your main residence again.

However, you can only claim this relief if no other residence qualifies for relief during the absence, i.e., you had no other nominated PPR.

John works as an IT consultant. As part of his employment contract, he works at different customer locations throughout the country.

He lives in North Wales, in a house he purchased in 1995 for £60,000. However, he is assigned to a long-term project in London in 1999.

His company provides him with rented accommodation in London, so he decides to live there for the duration of the project.

Because he will be vacating his house in North Wales, he decides to rent it out for an annual rental income of £5,000. He is liable to pay income tax on his rental profits.

John finishes his assignment in London and returns to his house in North Wales in January 2003. For the period 1999-2003, John informs HMRC that the two-bedroom house was his elected main residence.

After returning to North Wales he lives in his house for a year but then decides to move back to London on a more permanent basis.

His house is valued at £160,000 in February 2004. John will have no CGT liability because

- between 1995 and 1998 he lived in the property, so there is no CGT liability;
- between 1999 and 2003 the duties of UK employment required him to live elsewhere and there was no other property that was his PPR;
- from January 2003 to February 2004 he lived in the property, so there is no CGT liability.

31.4. CGT Implications of Providing Property to Dependent Relatives

There is no principal private residence relief available to an owner if he doesn't live in the property but his relatives do.

However, if someone owned a property on 5 April 1988 that has been continuously occupied rent-free by a dependant relative since that date, the property is exempt from CGT when the owner disposes of it.

Dependant relative is defined as the owner's own or the owner's spouse's widowed mother or any other relative unable to look after themselves because of old age or infirmity. There is another possibly tax effective way of providing a home for a relative: by acquiring a property, putting it into trust, and allowing the relative to live in it rent-free for life. However, this is a simplification of the subject, and professional advice must be sought.

32. Selling the Gardens or Grounds of Your Home

It is well known that if you make a gain when you sell a property that has been your "only or main residence" throughout your ownership of it, that gain will be exempt from capital gains tax ("CGT").

This exemption generally extends to the "garden or grounds" of the property, but there are several pitfalls to be aware of:

32.1. The "Permitted Area"

Up to half a hectare (1.24 acres) of grounds are automatically exempt. If your garden is bigger than this, you will need to persuade the taxman (in the shape of the District Valuer) that this larger area is "required for the reasonable enjoyment" of your residence, "having regard to the size and character" of the house.

The best evidence for this is likely to be the existence of similar houses nearby with similar gardens.

Where the grounds are more than half a hectare, and part of the garden or grounds are sold (perhaps to a developer) while the house and the rest of the garden are retained, HMRC will usually argue that the fact that you are prepared to go on living there after the sale shows you did not need the land sold for the "reasonable enjoyment" of your property.

The most likely ways to defeat this argument are if you can show that the sale was to a close friend or family member (on the basis that you were prepared to make a sacrifice to help them out), or that you were in need of cash and selling the land was the best way to raise it.

32.2. Location of Garden

HMRC will generally resist giving relief for a garden that is not part of the land on which the house is built, even if it is less than half a hectare in size. If you are a keen gardener with a small garden, but also own more land nearby which you also use as a garden, you are unlikely to get relief for that land.

The exception is where you can show that the land concerned is naturally part of the garden of the property, perhaps because it has been sold with the house on previous occasions.

There were some houses near where I used to live in London which had their gardens opposite them, across the road, and I have seen similar arrangements in some villages. These would be accepted as part of the garden of the house, and so exempt.

32.3. Timing of Sale of Garden

If you are selling your house and your garden to different purchasers, even if the garden is less than half a hectare, make sure you sell the garden before the house. This is because the test of whether it is your garden or not is done <u>at the time you sell it;</u> so if you have already sold the house, you cannot say it was in use as your garden at the time you sold it!

32.4. Use for Other Purposes

Where a house has been used for other purposes than as your home during your ownership, some of the gain may be taxable. The gain is time-apportioned between periods when the property was your main residence and when it was (for example) let out. This does not apply to the garden.

The test for exemption for the garden is a "snapshot" of the use of that garden at the time the property is sold, so if the garden is being used as the garden of your main residence at the time you sell it, all the gain on the garden is exempt, even if it has been used for other purposes during your ownership of it.

Conversely, if it is not being used as part of your garden at the time of sale, it will not qualify for relief, even if it has been part of the garden for most of the time you have owned the property.

32.5. Buildings on Land

If there is a building – say, a barn or a garage – in your grounds, then provided it is within the "permitted area", it will also be exempt as part of the garden or grounds of your main residence, provided it is not being used for some other purpose (such as being let, or used for your business) at the time you sell it.

If, for example, your half hectare of garden includes a garage you rent out to a neighbour, then if possible, stop renting it to him before you sell the house and garden, so that you qualify for the full exemption on the garden.

33. Understanding Inheritance Tax

Inheritance tax is becoming more and more of a 'tax bombshell.'

This is purely because property prices have increased so much over the past few years. If you do not plan for IHT now, then you could be passing on a huge tax liability as well as unwanted stress to your loved ones!

In this section you will become familiar with IHT and what you can do to minimise any future liability.

33.1. What is Inheritance Tax?

Inheritance tax is commonly referred to as a 'gift tax' or 'death tax.'

If at the time of your death you pass on part or the whole of your estate, then the inheritor could be liable to pay inheritance tax.

There is currently an IHT threshold level of £325,000 that has been effective since the 2011–2012 tax year. This nil rate band will be frozen, and will remain at £325,000 until the end of 2017/18. Anything above this amount is taxed at 40%, i.e., at the highest rate.

This means that if someone died after the start of the 2011-2102 tax year and the whole estate is valued at less than £325,000, the inheritor will have no inheritance tax to pay.

If the value of the estate is over this amount, then anything above the £325,000 will be taxed at 40%.

The March 2011 Budget announced that from April 2012, a reduced rate of IHT of 36% will be introduced where 10 per cent or more of the net estate is left to charity.

Please use the following link to view the IHT rates for previous years:

http://www.hmrc.gov.uk/rates/inheritance.htm

No IHT Liability

At the time of his death, John has an estate that is worth £240,000. His estate is made up of his house, which is worth £200,000, and the £40,000 cash in his savings account.

He gifts his entire estate to his son.

His son will have no IHT liability as it is below the threshold level.

Now, given the property price increases over the past few years, this threshold level seems to be *very low*.

If parents living in London, and the southeast in particular, were to pass away today, then it is highly likely that they would trigger an immediate tax liability on their loved ones.

This is because a very large number of properties in these areas are already valued at above the IHT threshold level!

The average property price in the United Kingdom in 2020 is predicted to be in excess of £330,000.

This means that more and more people are going to be subject to this tax liability in the future.

33.2. One VERY Important Point to Note!

If you die tomorrow and leave the estate to your children, then any IHT liability is due immediately by them.

IHT Due at Time of Death

Death befalls Albert. When Albert died, he left everything to his son.

At her time of death the estate is valued at £425,000. The son must pay £40,000 in taxes before he can take ownership of the estate.

This is because he is liable to pay tax at 40% on the £100,000 value of the estate that is above the £325,000 threshold level.

Now, in the above case study, if the estate was made up entirely from the value of the property, in which the son lived, then it may well be the case that the property will need to be sold in order to pay the tax liability!

Not only is there a significant tax burden, but there is also a huge inconvenience for the son.

33.3. FOUR Simple Ways to Reduce Inheritance Tax

There is no IHT liability if a spouse inherits assets from their partner. This is regardless of the value of the inheritance.

Here are four common ways of reducing inheritance tax.

a) Utilising the £325,000 threshold level
   If circumstances are such that your estate is not worth more than the current threshold level, then as mentioned earlier, there is no tax liability for the inheritor.

However, as we have seen earlier in this section, this scenario is becoming more and more unlikely!

b) Gifting to spouse

All gifts between husband and wife are exempt from tax as long as they are both domiciled in the UK.

This means that even if a husband has an estate valued at £10 million, then he can gift this to his wife.

It does not matter if it was gifted during his lifetime or at the time of his death; either way, his wife will incur no tax liability.

c) Gifting as soon as possible during your lifetime

During your lifetime, it can be tax beneficial to gift sooner rather than later. This is especially the case if you know who will inherit your estate.

If you gift during your lifetime, then your inheritor will be in possession of a potentially exempt transfer (PET).

A PET is a lifetime gift to an individual. If someone makes PETs amounting to any figure, then there is no lifetime IHT to pay, and if they survive for seven years after the last of those PETs, then there is no IHT to pay on death either.

> The longer you live, the less tax your inheritors will have to pay.

So, if you transfer a property or gift it away and survive for seven years, then the inheritor will have no IHT liability.

d) Trusts

You have already learned that husband and wife incur no IHT liability when gifting to each other.

However, if you want to gift to your children/relatives, then setting up a trust may be the best option.

Trusts can be used to hold properties as well as other appreciating assets such as stocks and shares.

Properties can be placed into trusts in a tax efficient manner, which can help to significantly reduce and even avoid capital gains or inheritance tax.

There are a number of different types of trusts that can be set up to make tax savings, and each have their own merits and are suitable for different scenarios.

It is strongly recommended if you are considering transferring to your children or other members of your family that you take tax advice from a tax expert.

33.4. Don't Forget Your Capital Gains Liability

> Your capital gains tax liability is not eliminated if you decide to gift/transfer a property.

If you decide to gift/transfer a property, then you are still liable to pay capital gains tax on any profit that *you* have made.

Timing of the transfer is crucial, and if you are not careful when you gift/transfer, then you might be hit with a CGT bill and your inheritor hit with an IHT bill.

Double Tax Liability

Alicia bought an investment property in April 1990 for £125,000, and in June 2009, it is worth £485,000.

She decides to gift the property to her son in her lifetime.

However, she soon changes her mind when it becomes evident that if she gifts it in her lifetime, the gift will trigger a significant tax liability on the £360,000 capital gain.

Instead, she takes tax advice on how to best limit her liabilities.

33.5. How to Avoid Inheritance Tax on Your Family Home

For most people, the family home is their most valuable asset. Unfortunately, it is also often the asset that admits them to what was once a very exclusive club – the Inheritance Tax club.

Inheritance Tax ("IHT") is charged on a person's "estate" (broadly, assets less liabilities) when they die. The first £325,000 is free of charge (the "nil rate band") and all the rest is charged at 40%.

Because the nil rate band has not kept pace with house prices, more and more people find themselves in line for what used to be a tax on the rich. Transfers between married couples (or civil partners) are exempt from IHT, so if the home is left to the surviving spouse there is no IHT cost on the first death, but when the survivor dies, the house may well have to be sold to pay the IHT.

Much ingenuity has therefore gone into schemes to avoid IHT on the family home, and these have been countered with much legislation.

There was a time when the ageing parent could simply "put the house in the children's names" and continue to live there – this has not been effective for many years, though sadly I still come across situations where people have thought it was, and get an unpleasant surprise when the parent dies and is still taxed on the value of the house.

The three biggest obstacles to IHT planning for the family home are:

- **"Reservation of benefit"** – If you give the house away, but carry on living there, you will be treated as if you still owned it for IHT purposes

- **"Life interests"** – If you do not own the property, but have the right to live there for the rest of your life, you are treated as if you owned it for IHT purposes

- **"Pre-owned Assets Tax"** – This is an annual charge to income tax on the "benefit" of using assets that you once owned in the past, or assets that you have never owned but which were bought by their owners with money that you gave them.

The tax on pre-owned assets began in 2005, but it catches arrangements made as long ago as 1986. Any future IHT planning might be similarly attacked with retrospective effect, so this is not a planning area for the faint-hearted!

Any IHT planning involving the family home needs expert advice, both to ensure that it works for tax purposes, and also that other vital factors are considered:

- Security for the person living in the house – some schemes rely on the generosity of the children in letting the parent occupy "their" house, but what happens if the children go bankrupt?

- The ability to move house in the future

- The potential problems if nursing home care becomes necessary (the rules on "deliberate deprivation" can deny local authority funding to those who have given assets away)

There are two sorts of planning to consider – lifetime planning, and "first death" planning.

33.5.1. Lifetime planning

The scope here is very limited – but the following can be considered:

- **Give away the home, then pay a full market rent to live there** - but the rent will be taxable income for the new owners of the home

- **Give a share in the home to (say) a child, who then lives there with you and shares the running costs** – but if the child moves out, the value of their share will be included in your estate again

- **Give cash to the children, wait seven years, then sell the house and move into one they buy with the cash** – this works, but only if you have that kind of cash available in the first place

- **Mortgage the house, and invest the money in assets that do not attract IHT, such as shares in unlisted trading companies (perhaps the children run such a company?), or agricultural land which is let out** – after two years, the investments described will qualify for 100% relief from IHT, and the mortgage will reduce the value of the house for IHT purposes – but you have to pay the mortgage interest. I have seen this work, but only because the parent concerned wanted to invest in the children's company anyway.

33.5.2. "First death" planning

If you are a married couple (or a civil partnership), there is some opportunity to pass the home down to the children when the first of you dies – a dead person cannot "reserve a benefit".

The first essential step is to ensure that you own the home as "tenants in common" rather than as "joint tenants". This is because a joint tenant inherits the other joint tenant's share automatically on their death, whereas a tenant in common can leave their share to whomever they wish. If you are joint tenants, it is a simple legal procedure to convert to being tenants in common.

Some planning possibilities on the first death are:

- **Leave your share of the house to the children** – this is the "low-tech" form of planning, and crucially, it relies on the children's generosity in allowing the surviving partner to live there undisturbed (they cannot evict him/her, but they could put a tenant in or force a sale of the property), and on them not going bankrupt. If the survivor wants to sell up and move, there will be capital gains tax to pay on the sale of the house.

- **Leave your share of the house to a "discretionary trust" with your partner and your children as beneficiaries** – assuming that your half of the property is worth less than the "nil rate band" there is no IHT to pay, and when your partner dies they can leave their share to the children as well. If, however, your partner wants to move, there may be CGT to pay when the house is sold, and there is a danger that HMRC will say that your partner has a "life interest" in the other half of the house. A more sophisticated scheme is:

- **Leave a cash legacy equal to the "nil rate band" to a discretionary trust, and empower that trust to take an index-linked charge over the house instead of cash** – this needs careful drafting to ensure that your partner does not have a "life interest" as before, and it is essential that the trustees of the trust know how to manage things to avoid this problem. The main advantage of this arrangement is that if the survivor wants to move house, they can do so without any CGT being payable on the sale of the old property.

It may be possible to deal with this planning after the first death, by using a "deed of variation" within two years of the death. This effectively rewrites the will, providing that the beneficiaries agree. IHT planning is a complicated business, and it is **essential** to get proper professional help. I will leave you with two pieces of advice:

- Make a will
- If someone tells you they know a "simple" way to avoid IHT, they do not understand how IHT works!

33.6. Other IHT Exemptions

33.6.1. Completely exempt

- Transfers between husband and wife; any transfers that take place between a husband and wife during lifetime and death are exempt from IHT.

- Gifts in consideration of marriage; it is possible for a parent to pay up to £5,000 to their child. The amounts that can be gifted by relatives and other friends are lower.

- Gifts to charities.

- Gifts for national purposes.

- Gifts to political parties.

33.6.2. Annual exemptions

- It is possible to gift up to £3,000 in any tax year.

- Certain trusts are also exempt from IHT.

33.7. NIL Rate Band for Surviving Spouse

The Chancellor in October 2007 announced that the second spouse in a marriage who dies is able to use the unused % of the nil rate band of the first spouse that died before them. This extra relief for the second spouse is automatic.

Nil Rate Band for Surviving Spouse

John and Jill have been married for 35 years. John dies in the 2008/2009 tax year and he leaves £156,000 to his children and the remainder to his wife Jill.

Because the nil rate band for 2008-2009 is £312,000 John has used 50% of his nil rate band. Jill dies in the 2010-2011 tax year when the nil rate band has increased to £325,000. She can use her own nil rate band plus the unused 50% from John. Therefore her total nil rate band that can be used is 150% * £325,000 which is £487,500.

Note: The second spouse inherits the % nil rate band unused by the first spouse. They do not inherit the actual amount in pounds unused. Therefore because John had only used 50% of his nil rate band, Jill is able to use an additional 50% of her nil rate band when she dies.

33.8. Inheritance Tax Uplift On The Main Home

This section has been written by Lee Sharpe.

A new additional Nil Rate Band for Inheritance Tax (IHT) was announced, which would increase each individual's tax-free estate to up to £1million – with further enhancements possible by virtue of the Transferrable Nil Rate Band (TNRB) between spouses / civil partners.

The measure is to be phased in over several years. Meanwhile, the standard Nil Rate Band (NRB) will remain at £325,000 per person until at least 2020/21.

The current IHT NRB means that basically the first £325,000 of one's net estate on death is free of IHT. Between couples, the first spouse to die can leave any unused NRB to the second; this tends to mean that it should be relatively straight forward to achieve £650,000 free of IHT on the joint net estate.

Ignoring special reliefs such as Agricultural or Business Property Relief, any excess net value will normally be taxed at 40% on death.

The problem for property investors is that the NRB has loitered around £325,000 for years, while property values march apace.

The Residential Nil Rate Band (RNRB) is an enhancement to the existing NRB such that those with a net estate of up to £1million (but basically not much more than £2million) can potentially benefit.

33.8.1. How Will it Affect Me?

The RNRB is potentially available to add up to £175,000 per person to the existing NRB and to reduce exposure to IHT so long as the claimant leaves at least one of their residences to a close relative. The additional element of the RNRB is tapered off at a rate of 50% once the value of the net estate exceeds £2million, so there is a chance that substantial estates will not benefit at all from this new measure (note the standard NRB is not tapered).

There is scope to transfer unused proportions of both the standard NRB and the RNRB element to the surviving spouse. As a couple, up to 2 x (£325,000 + £175,000) is available, which takes the aggregate net estate to potentially £1million free of IHT.

33.8.2. When Will it Affect Me?

The RNRB is being phased in as follows:

- 2017/18 £100,000
- 2018/19 £125,000
- 2019/20 £150,000
- 2020/21 £175,000

And thereafter to rise in line with inflation – the CPI – alongside the main NRB.

33.8.3. Practical Points

This measure will not start to protect £1million in property, etc., until 2020/21 – by which time portfolios will have increased even further in value.

There are welcome provisions in the legislation which protect the *value* of a previous, more valuable residence, even when someone down-sizes to a 'smaller' residence and it is that smaller property which is transferred on death.

33.8.4. What Should I Do?

This new RNRB will potentially protect additional value of up to £350,000 per couple. While it requires *a* residence to be transferred to a close relative, (a direct lineal descendant), it can still benefit property investors because the additional RNRB may be allocated to the residence, leaving more of the standard NRB(s) to cover investment properties. Investors should be looking to make sure that the deemed value of the residence is at least as much as the RNRB they are looking to utilise, to maximise IHT savings.

International Property Taxation

34. Essential Tax Advice for International Property Investors

34.1. About Daniel Feingold

Daniel is a Barrister who heads Strategic Tax Planning, a firm of Tax Lawyers Consultancy that has as one of its specialities UK and International Tax Planning for both high net worth individuals and corporate clients. This includes both structuring for UK clients investing in property abroad and UK property acquisitions for foreign investors. His advice is sought after by many accounting and law firms around the UK and overseas.

Daniel has over 31 years' experience specialising in tax law since qualifying as a Barrister in July 1983.

He has spent time at the Bar, in several leading City of London law firms and latterly in the International Tax Department of a leading accountancy firm, before establishing his own firm of Tax Lawyers.

Daniel is the lead international tax expert and a technical author for www.property-tax-portal.co.uk.

Daniel has written and lectured extensively on property tax planning; including the pitfalls of Spanish and French property investment and is a regular contributor to several publications on the whole spectrum of tax planning, especially avoiding capital gains on property sales.

Daniel is known as a 'creative' tax expert and has formulated his own unique tax mitigating solutions.

You can learn more about Daniel on-line at the following link:

➔ www.property-tax-portal.co.uk/consultancy_daniel.shtml

In the section below Daniel answers the most burning questions international investors have.

34.2. UK People Investing Outside the UK

For anybody investing overseas, what are the five most important tax considerations they need to make?

I would list these as follows:

'How is any capital gain on the property you are going to invest in going to be taxed in that country where you are investing in? Is there a withholding tax (which means that the country where the property is situated requires the purchaser to withhold a percentage of the purchase price and pay it over to the tax authorities?

How is any rental income going to be taxed? Is there a minimum tax on rental income? Is there a withholding tax (which means that the country where you get the rental income from somebody has to pay over a certain amount of tax to their tax authorities first)?

The third most important tax consideration is 'What Inheritance Tax will be levied on death or a gift of the property by the owner in that country where the property is situated? '

The fourth one I would say would be 'Are there any other local taxes to consider such as, purchase taxes when you buy a property, annual rates, (the equivalent of UK rates or council tax), and one that you probably won't have thought of is – annual wealth taxes, which are based on the value of a person's assets situated in that country?

And the fifth is to probably make sure that you know all the tax implications before you sign any legal binding agreement on the property.

If I invest overseas then when and where do I pay income tax?

With regards to income tax you will be liable to pay tax in the country where the property is situated. So for example if you have an investment property in Spain then you will be liable to pay tax in Spain.

It is important to note that you will also be liable to pay income tax in the UK on the rental income; however you will get a credit for any tax that you have to pay in the overseas country.

When does the tax year start and end in overseas countries?

Most overseas countries have a tax year that runs from the 1st January to the 31st December. This is very different to the UK tax year which runs from the 6th April to the 5th April.

What is a double taxation agreement?

These are agreements that are signed between the tax authorities of two separate countries. For example UK and France have a double taxation treaty. The objective of the treaty is to make sure that no income or gains or even other taxes are levied twice on the same portion of income.

So for example if you have a rental income of £10,000 on your property in France, then it should only be subject to income tax once as it would be unfair if this whole amount was taxed again in the UK.

Double taxation agreements are complex International Tax Treaties and you should seek professional advice about their application.

How can I use double taxation treaties to my advantage?

Well, this is difficult when it comes to property because property income tax and in fact the capital gains tax from properties are normally reserved under a double taxation treaty to the country where the property is located.

So it is really quite hard to get a benefit, although sometimes there are areas where for instance a limit can be put on how much tax on rental income can be levied. So for instance there could be a limited taxing right on rental income in the country where the property is, and so there would be a saving or benefit there.

Or they may reserve the right to tax the capital gain to the country to where the person is resident, and there could be a tax saving there.

So there are a few but very limited opportunities where a double taxation treaty can work to a person's advantage when investing in property.

My overseas property developer does not provide any tax advice, so should I therefore make it my own responsibility to seek professional advice before I invest or leave it until I decide to sell the property?

Unfortunately, this is an increasingly (and worryingly) growing trend amongst overseas property developers. The fact of the matter is that like any investment you should take advice from the outset, before you invest overseas.

The rush to jump onto the overseas property bandwagon leads to too many people not considering tax implications, until after they have purchased a property. Not only is this approach extremely high risk, but can also be very costly as well!

For example: In Italy, there is no Capital Gains tax after a property has been owned for more than 5 years but before that there is a rate of about 20% if you sell an Italian Property within 5 years of purchase. In the UK there will still be a liability to pay 28% when the property is sold regardless of length of ownership and the fact you have no Italian tax liability is irrelevant. (In the 2016 Finance Bill there is a proposal to cut the rate of UK Capital Gains Tax to 20% for every type of asset except residential property, where it will remain at 28%).

Can I choose which country I pay tax in? For example the tax rate may be cheaper in the country where I hold my overseas property.

No, not normally. If you are a UK resident and domiciled person (that is somebody who is born and brought up here) you will be liable to UK tax on your worldwide income and capital gains. You will also have to pay income tax and CGT in the country that the property is situated.

However, you need to remember that you will receive a tax credit against your UK tax liability for the tax that you have paid overseas.

Paying Tax in Two Countries

John (a UK Resident) buys an investment property in Spain for £300,000.

He rents it out for several weeks in the summer and receives £10,000 in rental income. His tenants (or the Spanish agent) should withhold 19% in 2016 if the rental income is paid to EU residents and 24% for anyone else less any deductions for expenses (A new law introduced in March 2010 will allow a deduction for expenses

---

for EU residents but only a portion that the rental period relates to the whole year. So, 7 weeks rental means 7/52 of expenses deductible! Another new law reduces withholding tax for EU residents to 19%) and pay that over to the Spanish tax authorities as his Spanish tax liability.

In the UK John will be able to deduct the Spanish tax charged at 19% from his UK tax liability charged at 40% (or 45% if the rental income places his income above £150k). If John is a UK basic rate tax payer or has put half the property in his wife's name and she is a basic rate tax payer, there will be 1% more UK tax to pay as they will have paid 19% in Spain but only liable to 20% in the UK.

John will be able to deduct any expenses in Spain such as agent's fees, repairs and mortgage interest.

Up to March 2010 John would have had to pay 24% of gross rents to the Spanish Tax Authorities meaning that his UK tax bill on the rental income was very small because in the UK he was allowed to deduct expenses.

There is an annual income tax based on the Spanish equivalent of the rateable value usually between 1.1% and 2% of the value of the property taxed at 19% that is payable whether the property is let and for periods when it is not let.

There is one other point that is probably worth mentioning for property investors. It may be possible, and this would be subject to advice on which specific country you are investing in, to form a local company and for that company to hold the property.

In such a case you may only have a liability to pay tax on the rental income in that country.

However this is subject to very careful tax planning advice.

If I sell a property abroad and pay the local taxes; I'm only liable for UK Capital gains tax when I bring the money back to the UK – Is that right?

Sadly no, this is a really old chestnut and many people make this mistake.

If you sell a property abroad and even if you have to pay local capital gains tax you are taxed within the UK on your world-wide gains as they arise. So even if you don t bring the money back into the UK, you still have to pay capital gains tax on that money.

If people misunderstand this and leave the money on deposit overseas; then there can be very serious consequences. For instance you could end up paying interest and even penalties to HMRC if you delay informing them about a capital gain on a property you have sold several years earlier.

I can give you a very good example of how this happens.

Many people sell their overseas properties when they have made a considerable gain. For instance I have many clients who are able to sell their property in Spain totally capital gains tax free because under a special law there a property purchased before a certain date avoids Spanish capital gains tax altogether, so they therefore paid no Spanish tax on sale.

They just deposited the money they received from the property into a bank account in Spain and assumed that there is nothing more they needed to do.

However, it is only when they contact somebody like myself a few years down the line and mention this point that they realise they have a tax problem.

If people have already made this mistake what should they do now?

I would recommend contacting a specialist UK tax adviser who can then inform HMRC and negotiate a settlement on your behalf, at the lowest tax cost. This will be under the Common Reporting Standard disclosure facility with a 30% penalty, but needs specialist advice.

If I sell my apartment abroad and buy a villa, surely I'll be able to rollover the gain I've made into the new villa and therefore I'll only need to pay Capital Gains Tax when I sell that in the future?

I am afraid that this is simply not true.

In the UK HMRC view investing in property as an investment and not a business. Roll-over relief is something specific to people who are in business.

For example if you have business premises from where you operate a business and then sell the premises and buy a bigger business premises, then you can roll-over the gain you have made. Now this can't be done with investment property in the UK, and it certainly can't be done with investment property abroad.

However there is one exception to this. Up to April 2012 if a property was in the European Economic Area and was available for let for 140 days and actually let for 70 days a year, excluding single lettings over 31 days, then it can qualify for roll-over relief. From 2012 the property must be available for let for 210 days and actually let for 105 days, a "period of grace" is to be introduced so that if for one or two years the new letting requirement is not met, the property can continue to qualify.

It is vital to make sure your property can qualify as this will be a valuable deferral of capital gains tax in the UK @ 28% or 10%. This needs specialist advice.

You often find in other tax systems: For example the system in the US, they allow a type of roll-over relief, and people spend a lot of time worrying about this trying to work out if they can get an advantage from it. But there is a problem. Even if the US allows roll-over relief; the UK does not (apart from the exception above).

Therefore, because you are taxed in the UK on the gains wherever you make them, if you sell a property in the US and try to use their roll-over relief on the gain you won't be allowed to use it for UK capital gains tax purposes, only for calculating US capital gains. This means that people will expend a lot of energy worrying about foreign roll-over relief when it is not going to affect their UK tax bill as they will still have the same overall liability.

Inheritance Tax overseas on the property is not a worry as I'll leave it to the wife in my will, so there's no tax to pay until she dies?

Unfortunately this is a terribly common misconception.

In UK tax law you have what is called a complete exemption if you leave your property to your spouse. In other words there is no tax to pay at that point.

In most European countries they have a very different approach to the law of inheritance. They have what is called 'Forced Heirship', which means that you have to leave your estate in equal proportions to your children and your wife.

Also there is only a very limited tax exemption for gifts between spouses and in some cases (such as Spain) as little as £15,000 can be left to your Spouse and after that you start to pay Inheritance Tax at sliding Spanish rates which depend on the closeness of the person receiving the gift.

So, it is something that causes a lot of people who have gone to live in Spain, (or people who have Spanish holiday homes), a lot of problems. This is because they suddenly get a shock when the spouse dies and they assume that there is nothing to pay. They will suddenly get a huge Spanish inheritance tax bill and they really haven't got very much in the way of other liquid assets/cash to pay the tax bill. This can often force them to sell the property triggering a further problem as they may have to pay capital gains tax as well. So, it can cause a lot of financial problems if this is not planned properly.

It is very important to get your planning right on this by taking combined specialist UK and Spanish tax advice. There are ways of getting round this problem by holding properties in a Company or creating a debt against the property but this must be done in advance with good advice, as it can create further UK and Spanish tax liabilities on transferring a property to a Company.

If I invest overseas, which tax authority needs to be notified that I own property? In other words do I need to inform the tax authorities in the UK and the overseas tax authority?

Assuming that there is rental income generated, then both tax authorities need to be informed. If you only buy a holiday home that is not rented, then initially only the tax authority in the country where the property is situated.

However, it is likely that sooner or later you will need to inform the UK Revenue & Customs as well.

34.3. Tax Advice for Ex-Pats

If I leave the UK to live and work in another country, but rent out my UK residence then am I liable to pay income tax?

Yes you have to pay UK income tax on your rental income. The amount paid can actually be up to the highest rate of UK income tax, which is currently 45% on income above £150k.

Furthermore, there is an obligation on the tenant, i.e. the person who has rented the property or on the estate agent who is handling the rental agreement, to withhold 20% of the gross rent from any money they pay over to you overseas.

There is a way out of this by having an agreement with HMRC. Such an agreement is the **Non Resident Landlord Scheme**. Once an agreement is reached with them, the rental income money can be paid to you (i.e. the landlord) without making the 20% deduction / commission.

Just to clarify if you have a Non Resident Landlord agreement then you would pay the tax on the usual dates under the self-assessment tax return. In order words you must declare the rent on your tax return and pay any tax due.

The other point to remember is that you may also have a tax liability on that rental income in the foreign country, where you have gone to live. Again, you will receive a credit for any UK tax you pay. However you will have an additional tax liability depending on the rules in that country.

If I leave the UK to retire abroad or live abroad permanently, what income tax and capital gains tax implications are there for my UK properties?

Firstly, you are still technically liable to pay income tax on your rental property profits. This often comes as a shock to many people. The reason why this is quite shocking to people is that some many believe that if you leave the UK and go and live abroad you are going to save UK tax. In fact, as far as rental income on property there is no saving whatsoever. E.g. if your rental income makes you a higher rate taxpayer you will have to pay UK income tax at up to 45%.

Secondly, capital gains tax will also be due if you decide to sell your UK properties once you have gone abroad. It is vital that you don't sell the properties until the UK tax year following the year in which you leave. So for example if you left the UK in January 2012 you must not exchange or sell that property until after April 6th2012.

Why can I not sell till April 6th2012?

This is because HMRC do not split tax years for capital gains or in fact income tax. If you are resident in the UK for any time after 6th April you are theoretically resident for the whole tax year. They only waive this rule by a special rule which is only really applicable for income and capital gains on earnings and assets acquired after you leave the UK.

Do I have to pay UK Capital Gains Tax if I sell my UK property?

From April 6th 2015 all investors in UK residential (not commercial property!) are liable for UK capital gains tax. The capital gains tax only applies to increases in value from that date. So, a valuation of the property at April 6th 2015 will be required to calculate any capital gains.

In relation, to avoiding capital gains that are due for prior periods then the following is still relevant. If you leave the UK permanently for at least five full UK tax years, starting from April 6th, then there is no UK Capital Gains Tax on selling your UK investment properties.

If you do return within that period, then you will have to pay the UK Capital Gains Tax in the tax year you return, though without interest.

Does this mean that I cannot return to the UK at all for the entire five years?

No, you can come back for anything between 16 and 182 days depending on the number of "Ties" you have with the UK. (Please note for this I am referring to returning to the UK and becoming treated as resident here). This is qualified by the new Statutory Residence Test which has a completely new set of tests based on "Ties" with the UK to establish if you have too many continuing connections with the UK.

How long am I treated as UK Domiciled, when I leave the UK to live somewhere else?

This is a complex question because it involves understanding what **Domicile** means.

Domicile basically means the country whose laws you choose to be governed by and where you consider your permanent home. If you leave the UK, sell all your properties and sever most of your connections with the UK, then you could theoretically be a Domicile in another country within a few years.

However there is an inheritance tax rule called **Deemed Domicile** which will basically tax you on your world-wide assets in the UK, until the end of the 4th tax year after leaving the UK.

So, even if you can move abroad permanently and sever sufficient connections with the UK and build up enough connections with your new country, you will still be subject to UK inheritance tax on your worldwide assets until the end of the 4th tax year after leaving the UK.

There are some double tax treaties and some tax planning that can override this rule, but they require specialist tax advice to take advantage of.

Is it true that my UK assets such as UK property will still be subject to UK Inheritance Tax, even if I'm considered Domiciled in another Country?

Yes, as well as having the Deemed Domicile rule, which keeps you in the UK inheritance tax net after you have left the UK, the UK treats any property physically situated in the UK as liable to UK inheritance tax. This is on the basis that it is situated in the UK. It actually doesn't matter where the person who owns it is domiciled.

The only relevant test is where the property is.

Is there any way of avoiding my UK inheritance Tax liability whilst I'm still Deemed Domiciled and Domiciled abroad if I keep my UK property?

Yes.

There are some measures you can put into place even during the Deemed Domiciled period to actually convert UK property, and any other assets you may have, into a special kind of property called **Excluded Property**.

This is too complicated to explain here but it is suffice to say that there is a solution that needs specialist advice.

One other method that people look at when they are domiciled abroad is to sell, or to transfer, their UK property to a non UK company and/or Trust. By doing this they can remove it from the UK tax 'net'. However Capital Gains Tax, Stamp Duty Land Tax and the Pre-Owned Asset Tax rules for inheritance tax need to be taken into account.

In the 2015-2016 tax year each individual has a UK inheritance tax allowance of £325,000.

Another simple planning method would be to gift a share in any UK property to your wife and children. By doing this you multiply the £325,000 allowance a number of times by the people in whose name you have the property. This will create a UK inheritance tax liability for seven years from the date of any gifts or transfers. However, this strategy requires specific advice.

What are your top three tax saving tips for Ex-pats?

Firstly, you should appoint a UK agent and apply to be taxed under the Non Resident Landlord scheme (NRL). This is essential if you want to avoid the 20% withholding tax.

Secondly, you need to consider ways to minimise the tax on UK rental income and avoid hitting the high tax bracket. You could again give a share of property to your wife or children, because each individual will then have UK rental income and will have the benefit of the personal allowance and also the lower tax bands. This can be a very valuable opportunity to save tax and avoid the 45% rate.

Thirdly, you need to establish how the rental income in the UK is to be taxed in the new country where you are re-locating. You need to know if it is going to be taxed in a beneficial way for you or whether you will be better off using an offshore or home country company.

34.4. Tax Considerations for People Investing in the UK

For overseas investors, what tax considerations should they make before investing in the UK?

First and foremost an overseas investor must get UK tax advice before they get to the exchange of contracts on any UK property. In other words, get appropriate tax advice before any legally binding documents are signed.

As a general rule, I would say that holding property in the UK in your own name is generally unattractive for tax reasons and its far better to hold it through an offshore company. If you find this out too late and you have already exchanged contracts, it can be very costly to then sell that property on, or transfer it on to an off shore company - especially from a UK stamp duty land tax perspective.

When does an overseas investor become liable to UK tax?

An overseas investor would be liable to UK tax from the point where they generate a rental income profit.

Again, it is back to the point I mentioned earlier with UK ex-pats, 20% tax would be withheld or ought to be withheld on the rent.

The investor needs to register for the Non Resident Landlord Scheme.

If the property has been bought in their own name then they could be liable to UK tax at up to 45%.

What can I do to minimise UK tax on rental income?

Form an Offshore Company.

Under the UK tax law any non-UK Company owning property in the UK can only be taxed on rental income up to a maximum of 20%. The basic withholding tax rate.

Investors have to pay Stamp Duty Land Tax on residential investment properties at up to 15% on residential properties worth more than £1.5 million. There are progressive scales that tax in bands from 3% above £40,000 through to the maximum 15%. This comes in on April 1st 2016 and follows new proposals in the 2016 Budget to further penalise investors in residential property.

However, if this is a residential property that is not rented out full-time to an unrelated 3rd party and is worth more than £2m then a new 15% SDLT charge on purchase, an annual ATED charge and UK Capital Gains Tax has been charged on gains from April 2013.

The definition of high value residential property is now going to be extended to properties worth more than £500,000.

The 15% SDLT charge will apply to transactions where the effective date (normally the date of completion) is on or after 20th March 2014; however, the ATED new charge will be phased in.

From 1 April 2015, where a property is worth between £1 million and £2 million, an ATED charge of £7,000 per year will apply. In addition, CGT on the ATED related gains will apply from this date.

From 1 April 2016, where a property is worth between £500,000 and £1 million, an ATED charge of £3,500 will apply. In addition, CGT on the ATED related gains will apply from this date.

Investors not renting out to close family need NOT be concerned with these changes. (There is also a separate capital gains tax regime known as ATED capital gains which applies capital gains on such properties from as early as April 2012).

Unfortunately, from April 2015 Non-UK Investors in residential property in the UK will face a new capital gains tax charge.

This will levy UK capital gains tax on any increases in value from April 6th 2015 and represents a significant change and is aimed at discouraging new investment in UK residential property by non-Residents.

If a property has been purchased a year or more earlier, it will be worthwhile seeking advice and obtaining a formal valuation at that date to support any claims as to the value and minimise any UK capital gains tax going forward.

<u>Remember! UK commercial property, such as shops and offices will NOT be subject to UK capital gains tax for Non-UK investors.</u>

Specialist advice will be needed if the investors ends up occupying a residential property, or its not let out full time, or a related party or relative ends up as the tenant.

If the Company has to take out a loan to acquire the property, then it is entitled to deduct the interest on that loan. The rules are such that you can actually loan your own money to your off offshore company and get a deduction from that. Again, this needs careful planning.

What can I do to make sure my Profit on selling a property is treated as a Capital Gain and therefore tax-free?

To guarantee a UK property is not going to be subject to UK capital gains tax it must be held as a pure investment.

A non-resident investing in UK property will not be subject to UK capital gains tax unless the property has been re-furbished or developed in any way. A property must be held as an investment for at least one year, so that there is at least one-year's rental income. Please note that this *one-year rule* is not derived from any official ruling. It is just a rule that has been developed by experience from practitioners dealings with HMRC on this issue and could be attacked if HMRC believe that there was an intention to sell on ASAP from the beginning.

Non-UK residents selling UK property

Alice is resident in Barbados. She decides to buy an investment property in London. The property is purchased for £250,000 and she rents it out at £2,000 per month. She holds the property for two years and then decides to sell it for £300,000 in February 2015.

She will not be liable to pay any UK capital gains tax as the property was held purely for investment purposes and was sold before April 2015. If sold instead in February 2016 she may have had to pay some small amount of UK capital gains tax based on the increase in value form April 2015!

Barbados does not have any capital gains tax and so the profit is totally tax-free.

So as an overseas investor, I'm not liable for UK Capital Gains Tax when I sell my investment property, am I?

This is broadly correct for commercial property such as shops and offices. For residential property, there is capital gains tax on any increase in value from April 6th 2015.

Another potential problem is highlighted below where a UK property (be it residential or commercial) is not held merely as an investment.

However it is vital that the property has been held for investment and there has been no significant development work. Again we come back to having at least one-year rental income and also not carrying out any significant development on the property.

If there was significant development on it then there is a potential that the gain could be taxed as UK income so it could be taxed at up to 45%.

Is it true as an overseas investor that I am liable for UK Inheritance Tax on my UK properties?

Yes I am afraid that this is back to the rule in UK tax laws where inheritance tax is levied on the basis of where the property is situated.

A property in the UK held by an overseas investor will still be subject to UK inheritance tax.

Is there a simple way to avoid UK Inheritance Tax?

Yes.

The key rule is that you should not hold a property directly (i.e. in your own personal name) but you should invest via a non-UK (possibly an Offshore) Company whose share register is kept outside the UK.

If this is the case then there is no UK inheritance tax on the asset. This is because it is held in a foreign company and the asset that you hold are actually foreign Company shares. This means that the shares are not classed as UK property.

This will therefore allow you to keep the asset outside of the UK inheritance tax net.

Again, in the context of UK residential property another radical change and disincentive is about to be introduced. So, the long standing exemption of holding property via a non-UK Company is about to change. Proposed new rules will be introduced on April 6th 2017 subjecting all UK residential property held by non-UK individuals or other entities such as Companies to UK Inheritance Tax.

In the case of non-UK Companies this will be based on the underlying beneficial owner of the company. One way to mitigate these effects is to place the non-UK companies shares in an Offshore Trust. This will limit the UK Inheritance Tax charges to special 10 year and exit charges at a maximum rate of 6%. This may be preferable to the current 40% UK Inheritance Tax on assets worth more than £325.000. Again. one for specialist advice. Once again, this does not apply to commercial property.

As an overseas investor, I've been offered the chance to invest in a UK property development. Is the taxation any different? Surely, I'm not liable to UK Capital Gains and so the profits are UK tax-free?

The minute you move from just buying a property to hold as an investment to carrying out development work or trading, buying & selling property then, there is a risk that you can be taxed in the UK with income tax up to 45%.

This is a very complex area and it involves a special anti-avoidance provision in UK tax law.

If someone was considering not just investing in the UK but participating in a UK development then there are two planning measures they should look in to.

First of all, by using double taxation treaties with various locations it may be possible to avoid the potential application of this section and ensure that any profits on the property are treated as **business income or trading income** and not taxable in the UK.

This is subject to some complex new provisions in the Finance Act 2008.

Another simple tip in this area is that if there is substantial risk that you are going to carry out some development in a property then you might want to consider involving a UK Company and letting that company pay tax on the development gains. If you do this, then you will be outside the scope of the special anti-avoidance provision.

Also, if the Company is making profits up to £300,000 in the UK then it is only going to be subject to corporation tax at 20% from April 2015 (whatever the level of profits) which represents a considerable saving on income tax of up to 45%.

34.5. Summary

Is there one final point you would like to make?

I really believe that from my experience too many people invest abroad and get very emotionally involved with the idea of purchasing a property abroad. They don't look into the tax aspects or any other relevant practical aspects before they go ahead.

Very often there are either other locations where you can buy a property with far less tax complications, or there is planning you can do before you buy a property.

In many cases it may be worthwhile considering buying a property not through your own name but through a company- either a local company in Spain or for instance a local company in France such as the Society Civil Immobliere (SCI).

It might also be worth considering using a UK company. There is no one simple or stock solution and everyone's objectives, family circumstances etc. have to be considered.

My key advice would be to factor in as part of your purchase the investment in specific tailored tax advice before you buy a property. This is because once the property is registered in your name, it is much harder to do any tax planning.

35. How to Better manage Your Property Taxes

A message from Amer Siddiq, founder of:

Property Portfolio SOFTWARE

www.propertyportfoliosoftware.co.uk

When I began investing in property, I naturally looked around for a software solution to help me to get better organised. I quickly realised that there was nothing suitable available and so I designed my own tool based on my personal experiences and input from other very experienced landlords.

My aim was to design an easy to use solution to overcome the five biggest property management challenges faced by landlords with growing portfolios:

- Getting better organised: cutting the time spent handling paperwork

- Staying legal: keeping track of safety certificates and legal documents

- Tenant management: accurately tracking tenant payments

- Income tax management: Knowing what is due and when

- Maintaining and growing a positive cashflow

Landlord &Letting AWARDS
2010/11 & 2011/12

Get better organised today with the UK's No1 award winning property management software solution.

Landlords Property Manager is the result - the award winning solution on the market that is the only official landlord software recommended by the Residential Landlords Association (RLA) and is the recognised software tool for the National Landlords Association (NLA).

Features include:

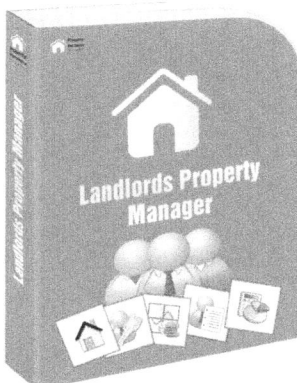

Property Manager - Fast management and full control of all property management tasks. Accurately track all property related income and expenditures.

Early Warning System - Generates reminders and notifies you of outstanding rental or loan payments.

Tenant Manager - Manage your tenants, track your rental income and produce your legal documents. You can also upload and store your own documents within the software itself, helping you keep organised.

Finance Manager - Central control of all your mortgages and property related loans.

Income Tax Calculator - The only solution on the market that also calculates your rental income tax.

Report Manager - Over 15 one-touch property management reports to help you analyse your portfolio, including Profit and Loss, Cash Flow Analysis and Portfolio Income Assessment.

Support Manager - A wealth of support resources to keep you running night and day. Gives you one click access to support resources from within the software.

To learn more about our powerful and easy to use property management software for landlords, visit:

**Property
Portfolio
SOFTWARE**

www.propertyportfoliosoftware.co.uk

If you prefer landlord software that runs 'in the cloud' then visit our new brand:

landlord vision

www.landlordvision.co.uk

Good Advisors Do Save You TAX!

36. Finding an Accountant

There is a saying, "a good accountant pays for him/herself". Never a truer word has been spoken.

In this chapter we will become familiar with and understand how to acquire the services of an excellent accountant.

36.1. Accountants Qualifications

The first step is to ensure that your accountant is a member of a recognised institute.

Some of the popular ones amongst accountants are ACA, ACCA, ICAEW, ICAS etc.

Here is what these abbreviations stand for:

- Association of Chartered Accountants (ACA)
- Association of Chartered Certified Accountants (ACCA)
- Institute of Chartered Accountants in England and Wales (ICAEW)
- Institute of Chartered Accountants in Scotland (ICAS)

Furthermore it would not be a bad idea to pick an accountant who is a member of the Chartered Institute of Taxation or Association of Taxation Technicians.

Getting to know the history of your proposed accountant is a very good idea, so look for the following signs:

a) Are they a former Tax Inspector?
b) Have they passed the Taxation (ATII, ATT) exams?

A qualified tax advisor is useful for all sorts of tax related services and these include:

- Preparing tax returns
- Sole trader tax returns
- Tax planning advice

It is most likely that your tax advisor will charge on an hourly basis. However some will agree a flat fee beforehand.

It is pertinent to ask whether one should go for a general or specialist tax advisor, although it may seem better to go with the general advisor as he/she will most definitely be cheaper.

However in the long-term the specialist may save you money because of his/her in depth knowledge and experience.

36.2. General Advisor or Tax Specialist?

A specialist will have the answer, usually to hand, whereas a non-specialist may have to consult HMRC documentation or may indeed consult the specialist and then pass the charge back on to you.

Cost can be a significant issue as a specialist can charge around £270 per hour. For this you get about 15 minutes of quizzing followed by 45 minutes worth of (in most cases) written response (Oh and that's plus VAT!)

To put that into perspective a non-specialist can charge around £150 per hour. A typical session with a non-specialist can take up to 2.5 hours. This time would be typically spent in the following way:

- 15 minutes of clarification.
- 1.5 hours of research.
- 45 minutes of written response.

As you can see sometimes it is beneficial if you go direct to a specialist, particularly if your questions to your accountant require him/her to study before responding.

With the above two examples in mind it is important to ascertain a working relationship with your advisor. You should be familiar with his/her area of expertise and know what their limitations are i.e. what they are not too hot on.

36.3. How to Choose Your Adviser

Before you sign up with a tax adviser or accountant, be sure to address the following:

36.3.1. Will I need a tax adviser or an accountant?

More often than not people will actually require both, however, it is important to establish why you need them- do you need someone to manage your accounts and help you with your tax return, or someone to give you sound advice that will legally save you money. Your accountant can manage your accounts, provide compliance work and some may even do tax planning.

However, tax advisers tend to focus solely on tax planning. They spend significant amounts of time keeping up-to-date with the latest tax legislation and tax cases to help make sure they provide their clients with great strategies that will help to reduce or eliminate tax - some of which your accountant may not even be aware of!

If we compare the accountancy profession with medicine, an accountant is the equivalent of a GP, and most of the time a GP is all you need for routine health care, but if you get seriously ill (compare with a dispute with HM Revenue and Customs) or you need surgery (tax planning), then you need a specialist consultant (a Tax Adviser).

36.3.2. What qualifications?

As a client you want to be assured that your tax adviser / accountant is acting in both your best interest and within the law, which is why it is important to know what qualifications your tax adviser or accountant has, and when they were achieved and if they are relevant to you. Check that the qualifications they have cover the area of taxation or accounting that you require assistance with.

36.3.3. How much experience do they have?

When choosing a tax adviser or accountant, it is good to know just how much experience they have and what their reputation is.

Do not be afraid to ask how long have they been giving advice, where they worked before or if they have ever done any public speaking or written work that you can refer back to? Another good question to ask is how many existing clients they have within the area that you are interested in, for example – if you develop property, how many other developers have they provided advice for and will they be able to provide references?

Good advisers will boast about their success, so give them to the opportunity to do so!

36.3.4. How much will it cost?

That really does depend on what type of advice or service you require. The fees generally reflect the adviser's / accountant's level of experience and qualifications, along with the amount of time they may have to spend on your case; in this instance you can request an estimate of the total. Also ask when fees need to be paid by.

Some accountants and tax advisers do offer 'fixed fees' for certain types of advice or help so that you know exactly what you are paying and exactly what you will receive.

Try to negotiate a fixed fee wherever possible, as good advisers won't be afraid to operate on this basis. It is far better than the 'let the clock run' approach, though in some cases such as a tax investigation, hourly charges are the only practical way to work.

36.3.5. Professional bodies

There are various professional bodies that you will find tax advisers and accountants to be part of.

Anybody who claims to be able to give 'tax advice' should be a 'Chartered Tax Adviser' (CTA), which means that they will be member of the Chartered Institute of Taxation and will have taken and passed their examinations.

Qualified accountants will have Chartered Certified Accountant (ACCA or FCCA), or Chartered Accountant (CA, ACA or FCA) in their title.

36.3.6. What about indemnity cover?

If an adviser gives you inappropriate advice or your accountant does not manage your accounts correctly it could result in a huge financial loss for you.

Finding out at the beginning what indemnity cover a tax adviser or accountant has will mean peace of mind for you. Find out whether they are covered for loss of documents, court attendance and legal fees, breach of confidence or misuse of information to suggest just a few areas. Ask who they are covered by and for how much per claim.

Knowing what protection your adviser or accountant has will protect you. You will be alarmed to learn that some advisers do not even have indemnity cover and you are well advised to stay away from such advisers. Chartered accountants and Chartered Tax Advisers are required by the rules of their professional bodies to have professional indemnity insurance.

36.3.7. How do I contact my tax adviser / accountant?

It can be quite frustrating when each time you phone your tax adviser or accountant they are unavailable.

Find out in advance how to contact them and if this suits you.

If you have 'ad-hoc' questions to ask your adviser or accountant and you cannot reach them, how soon will they get back to you? Also, find out if they are happy to receive email as you may prefer this method of correspondence.

Your chosen advisers should personally respond to your enquiries and calls within an agreed timescale.

A recent development has been the growth of online accountants and tax advisers, and if you do not feel the need for face to face contact with your adviser, you may want to consider using such a firm. Having lower overheads in the form of offices and meeting rooms, they are often able to offer lower fees than the conventional firms.

36.3.8. Keep up to date with tax legislation changes

Tax legislation is constantly changing. That is why it is important that your adviser or accountant keeps up-to-date with all the changes.

Also, to retain their qualifications, tax advisers and accountants must adhere to on-going training programmes enforced by their regulatory bodies, to ensure that they are keeping abreast of the latest changes in legislation and the latest tax planning opportunities.

For Example, CPD (Continuing Professional Development) is the compulsory training a Chartered Tax Adviser is required to do each year in order to keep his qualifications. He or she must do a minimum of 90 hours training per year; broken down into at least 20 hours "structured" training - that is, attending seminars, lectures, etc., and 70 hours "unstructured" training (such as reading textbooks and technical articles)

36.3.9. What if I have an emergency?

You are now aware of how to contact your tax adviser or accountant but what happens if you have an emergency and need urgent tax advice?

How easily to contact are they in a crisis?

Knowing that you can rely on the tax adviser or accountant is an important point when considering their services. Make sure that you are able to contact them without having to arrange a formal meeting!

36.3.10. Does the adviser sell 'off the shelf' solutions/schemes?

This is a very important question to ask your adviser. There are certain advisers out there who sell tax schemes (also known as 'off the shelf' tax solutions) and earn significant amounts of commission by doing so.

If your adviser mentions such schemes to you, then be cautious as HM Revenue and Customs are getting tough on such schemes, and legislation has been introduced requiring those using them to disclose the fact to HMRC.

37. A Final Reminder - The Golden Tax Rules

The challenge to you as a property investor will no doubt be how to grow a profitable portfolio. One of the easiest ways you can make money in property is to pay less tax.

37.1.1. Education…education…education

Whether you are starting out in property investing or are an experienced landlord with a sizeable portfolio, there is one thing that you should always do - educate yourself to make sure you are:

a) complying with the ever changing legal requirements

b) learning how to make your investments more profitable

c) making sure you keep up-to-date with tax changes that may affect your tax liability.

Although there is never a substitute for taking professional advice, you should keep yourself updated so that you can discuss these opportunities with your adviser at your next appointment.

37.1.2. Prevention is better than cure

There is a proverb 'prevention is better than cure' (believe it or not this was first said by the famous medieval philosopher Erasmus) and he probably was not thinking about tax when he said it, but it most certainly applies.

Planning for a tax situation you are likely to face is much better than trying to get out of a tax problem that you have unknowingly (or even knowingly) fallen into. It is certain that trying to get out of a tax problem will cost much more in specialist/consultancy fees and there is never a guarantee that you will get out of the problem.

Congratulations – You've now finished How to Avoid Landlord Taxes'

To learn even more ways on how to legitimately cut your property tax bills please visit: www.property-tax-portal.co.uk.

Lightning Source UK Ltd.
Milton Keynes UK
UKOW07f2006201216
290441UK00003B/40/P

9 780993 251320